IMAGES OF WAR

WORLD WAR TWO AT SEA
THE LAST BATTLESHIPS

RARE PHOTOGRAPHS FROM WARTIME ARCHIVES

PHILIP KAPLAN

Pen & Sword
MARITIME

First printed in Great Britain in 2014 by
Pen & Sword Maritime
an imprint of
Pen & Sword Books Ltd.
47 Church Street
Barnsley,
South Yorkshire
S70 2AS

A CIP record for this book is available from the British Library

ISBN 978 1 78303 638 7

Printed and bound in England
By CPI Group (UK) Ltd. Croydon, CRO 4YY

Pen & Sword Books Ltd incorporates the Imprints of Pen & Sword Aviation, Pen & Sword Family History, Pen & Sword Maritime, Pen & Sword Military, Pen & Sword Discovery, Wharncliffe Local History, Wharncliffe True Crime, Wharn-cliffe Transport, Pen & Sword Select, Pen & Sword Military Classics, Leo Cooper, The Praetorian Press, Remember When, Seaforth Publishing and
Frontline Publishing.

For a complete list of Pen & Sword titles please contact
Pen & Sword Books Limited
47 Church Street, Barnsley, South Yorkshire, S70 2AS
England

E-mail: enquiries@pen-and-sword.co.uk
Website: www.pen-and-sword.co.uk

Contents

Early Efforts

"Warships" of various types have taken part in battles at sea for many centuries, but it was not until the introduction of cannon as the main armament of such vessels in the fifteenth century that modern battleships began to evolve. But such ships "of the line of battle" remained under sail and as such relatively limited in capability until the latter part of the nineteenth century and the advent of steam power.

Until the late nineteenth century, the warships of the world's great navies were assembled in formations known as lines of battle. When these lines of ships from opposing forces met in combat, they sailed as a line, parallel with or at an angle to a similar formation of their opponent, thus bringing their considerable rows of cannon to bear on their enemy's vessels. These ships of the line of battle began to be referred to as battleships. They were the major or capital ships of their navies.

"Borne each by other in a distant line, / The sea-built forts in dreadful order move; So vast the noise, as if not fleets did join, / But lands unfixed, and floating nations strove. / Now passed, on either side they nimbly tack; / Both strive to intercept and guide the wind; / And, in its eye, more closely they come back, / To finish all the deaths they left behind." —from *Annus Mirabilis* by John Dryden

The evolution of the modern capital ship got under way at Portsmouth, England, with the sailing of the Tudor warship *Mary Rose* in 1511, the earliest true warship of the Royal Navy, the navy of King Henry VIII, and named for his favourite sister. The oak and elm-built *Mary Rose* had a waterline length of 127 feet, a beam of thirty-eight feet and a draught of fifteen feet. She was manned by a crew of about 400, and was armed with breech-loading guns made of wrought iron and muzzle-loading guns

below: The English King Henry VIII and, below right, the *Mary Rose*, the earliest true warship of the Royal Navy, named for the king's favourite sister; left: A USS *Penssylvania* sailor writing home.

left: HMS *Victory* was commanded by Vice Admiral Horatio Nelson, and is preserved in Portsmouth Dockyard; below left: Nelson, in a portrait by Charles Lucy; below: The French warship *Cordiliére* burns in a battle with the English fleet of Admiral Edward Howard, whose flagship was then the *Mary Rose*.

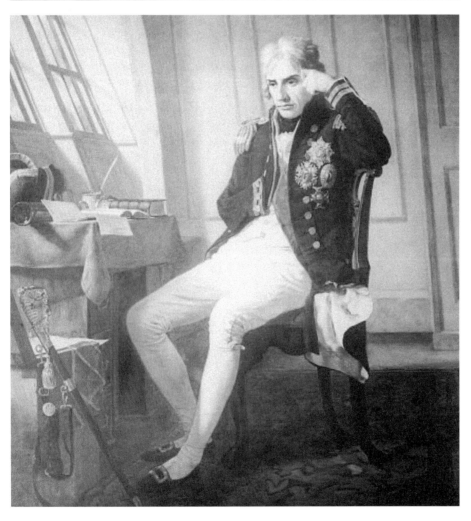

of cast bronze, by some of the world's best gun-founders, brought over from France by Henry, who also employed a number of highly skilled bowmen on board. It was their task to kill the crewmen of enemy vessels. The *Mary Rose* was, unlike most of the warships of the Royal Navy at the time, designed from scratch as a fighting vessel. Much of her design, and the way in which she was equipped, included substantial input from the king himself, who was determined that she lead the field in state-of-the-art capability and outfitting for her duties in the defence of England against all real and theoretical enemies. She was the prototypical battleship, and among her many innovative characteristics was the placement of her big guns in a long row down each side of her hull, near to the waterline, allowing her gunners to fire heavy broadside barrages at enemy ships. It was an inventive alternative to the naval tradition to date of mounting the guns on the 'castles' at both ends of the hull. *Mary Rose* also was constructed with her deck planking laid down edge to edge in a Carvel-type layout, making her hull more watertight.

It was in the autumn of 1511 that the Pope joined the King of Aragon in an alliance against Louis XII of France. The next year the English Parliament allied Britain with Spain and *Mary Rose* was readied to serve as the flagship of Admiral Edward Howard in the lead of twenty-five warships attacking the mighty French fleet at Brest on 10 August. Howard faced 222 French fighting vessels in a two-day battle. He began by striking at the French flagship, *Grande Louise* under the command of Vice Admiral René de Clermont who was unready for the arrival of Admiral Howard's fleet, which he had been expecting several days later. He had been raiding French and Breton vessels, including fishing boats, along the Brittany coast in late July. When Howard's ships appeared, many of the French naval officers and men were on shore celebrating the Feast of St Lawrence. In another odd turn of events, Hervé de Porzmoguer, captain of the French warship *Cordeliére*, had invited his family, together with about 300 local citizens, to a party aboard his ship, and as the English warships approached, Captain Porzmoguer had to accept the fact that he and his crew would have to fight the English with his passengers and guests aboard. Admiral Howard quickly assessed the situation and, seeing the considerable advantages he held, acted immediately to attack the *Grande Louise*. The heavy cannon of the *Mary Rose* soon destroyed the mainmast of the French warship, panicing a number of the French seamen and officers, many of whom retreated with their vessels towards Brest. With the final shots of the struggle at the end of the second day, Howard's force had captured thirty-two of the French warships and 800 of their seamen.

Over the ensuing years, the English king continued campaigning the *Mary Rose* and applied considerable planning, effort and funds to the fortification of the southern English coastal approaches in preparation for possible French attacks. One such effort was the installation of a great chain boom at Portsmouth extending to the Gosport shore to close off the harbour entrance. But by spring 1545, the French fleet was threatening to launch a major attack on Henry's key naval base at Portsmouth. They were determined to eliminate the king's warships in their anchorage there. Little transpired until 18 July, when the French warships anchored near the Isle of Wight. With his enemy now in English waters, Henry anticipated their landing at Portsmouth. He had prepared for their coming and the deepwater channel was protected by the Round and Square Towers as well as the Southsea Castle gun batteries. His vessels were further protected by the presence of the dangerous shallows near the harbour entrance. The king awaited the French naval forces with a significant force of his own—100 warships and 12,000 able men. His French enemy, however, had brought a fleet of some 225 galleys and warships crewed by 30,000 men. A day after Henry's fleet sailed from the Portsmouth harbour to meet the French, only a few mostly minor clashes had occurred by nightfall. The next dawn brought a calm sea as the French captains took their vessels into action. In that encounter, *Mary Rose* was lost. According to a French account of the incident, she was struck by cannon fire, heeled over and sank. An English version differs, suggesting that, as *Mary Rose* hoisted sail in preparation for getting under way, she suddenly heeled as she came about. With her gunports open and her cannon run out on their mounts for action, seawater rushed in over the gunport sills as she heeled, destabilising her and causing her to capsize and sink rapidly.

Overall, this Anglo-French sea encounter proved inconclusive, with *Mary Rose* being the only important casualty. From that day until 1982, attempts to raise her failed. Then, when she had finally been brought up from the seabed, her wreck was taken back to the dockyard where she had been constructed. In the two centuries after she went down, the great naval powers of the world—Britain, France, Spain, Portugal and the Netherlands had created vast colonial empires and great naval fleets to protect them. Comparatively, the other colonial empire nation's warship fleets of vessels were bigger, faster and more stable on the high seas than those of the British. The British, though, possessed the advantages of superior gunnery skills, greater discipline, and better training overall. They took and held the lead among the world's great naval powers until the time of America's War of Independence, in which the French took the side of the Americans against Britain. Spain then sided with France, threatening the possibility of a two-pronged attack against England. It marked the beginning of the decline of the Royal Navy and the British were defeated by the Americans in 1783, marking the end of three centuries of Royal Navy dominance at sea.

Next in the line of great British warships was HMS *Victory*, flagship of the Viscount, Vice Admiral Horatio Nelson who commanded a crew of 850 men. Sheathed in copper, *Victory* was 226 feet long, with a fifty-two-foot beam and a draught of twenty-one feet. She was armed with 102 cast-iron cannon, from twelve to thirty-two pounders along with two sixty-eight pounders. In the early part of the nineteenth century *Victory* headed the British fleet in the Mediterranean and Atlantic with the aim of drawing the French fleet into combat.

By 1793, Napoleon Bonaparte was engaged in military activities in Europe, underscoring the potential for a possible Franco-Spanish invasion of Britain. Under orders from Napoleon in 1804, Admiral Pierre-Charles Villeneuve's assignment was to take his fleet of eleven ships of the line from the port of Toulon, past the British blockade in the English Channel and, in a prelude to Napoleon's planned invasion of Britain, draw off the British defences by sailing across the Atlantic to the West Indies and there join with the Spanish fleet and French warships out of Brest to attack some of Britain's Caribbean possessions. Thereafter, they were to proceed back to the English Channel to destroy Britain's channel squadrons before escorting Napoleon's troops into England.

After some delays, Admiral Villeneuve finally left Toulon, evading the British blockade, and crossing the Atlantic with Nelson's ships chasing him, approximately a month behind owing to unfavourable winds. When Villeneuve's ships reached the island of Martinique, he was forced to waste a month awaiting the arrival of the other French fleet from Brest, also delayed. Under considerable French Army pressure to open the planned attack on the British, he raided and recaptured the Diamond Rock fort off Martinique. Nelson's fleet finally arrived at Antigua on 7 June. The next day Villeneuve's ships intercepted fifteen British merchant ships which were being escorted by two warships. In the encounter, the two escorts escaped as the French fleet proceeded to capture the entire convoy with an estimated value of five million pounds. 11 June. Villenueve and his fleet departed the Caribbean for

The all iron-hulled HMS *Warrior*, completed in 1862, was faster and better armed than the French warships of the time. She carried a blast furnace in her boiler room to produce molten iron for the making of hollow shot.

HMS WARRIOR

Europe, once again with Nelson's warships in pursuit. By 22 July, Villeneuve's combined Franco-Spanish force, now numbering twenty ships of the line accompanied by seven frigates, reached Cap Finisterre and sailed into the Bay of Biscay where they met a fifteen-warship British fleet under the command of Vice Admiral Robert Calder. The two fleets engaged each other in appalling visibility. The action resulted in the capture of two Spanish vessels by the British. Then, against orders, the French commander set sail for Cádiz, a move which wrecked Napoleon's intended invasion of Britain.

Napoleon's naval force then headed for Naples where they were to support an action against Italy. Early in the morning of 20 October, Nelson's warships lay in wait for the fleet of Villeneuve and French Contre-Admiral Charles René Magon de Médine in the Straits of Gibraltar off Cape Trafalgar. The next day would bring one of the final great open-sea battles of the age of sail.

Nelson used the occasion to try a new tactic he had developed. He formed his warships into two distinct parallel lines at a 90 degree angle to the enemy line, causing the French and Spanish ships to scatter, giving his own captains superior engagement opportunities in the ship-to-ship actions. Though more risky than the standard Admiralty tactics of engagement, Nelson believed the added risk worthwhile. He thought the Spanish and French gunners relatively unskilled and poorly trained, with less than one-third the capability of his own gunners.

By the late morning of the 21st, the cannon of Victory had been made ready for the day's action. The sea was calm with little wind and the British warships were quite slow in their approach to the enemy vessels. At 11:30 Nelson sent his famous 'England expects' flag signal to his fleet, together with

left: John Ericsson, inventor of the innovative warship of the American Civil War, the USS *Monitor*; upper right: A contemporary lithograph of the battle between the *Monitor* and the CSS *Virginia* [*Merrimac*], in March 1862; right: Officers and the turret of the *Monitor* after the three-hour gunfight with the *Virginia* in Hampton Roads near the entrance to the Chesapeake Bay.

'Engage the enemy more closely'.

As Nelson's ships closed in on those of his enemy, his opponents began firing at his ships, checking the range which was by then quite short. Now cannon balls were striking *Victory* and killing members of her crew. As *Victory* slid between the French flagship and another enemy vessel, *Victory*'s gunners sent a broadside into the French flagship sufficiently powerful to kill or injure nearly 400 crewmen. As late afternoon came, the sea battle wore down, leaving the British triumphant, but also suffering the loss of their commander, Admiral Nelson, who was mortally wounded by a French sniper. His fleet had shown itself to be well-led, highly-trained and disciplined. It had faced and defeated an opponent whose vessels were faster and better armed. The Trafalgar battle served to re-establish the Royal Navy in the role of the world's dominant naval force. After Trafalgar, the British fleet sailed wherever it chose to go, virtually unchallenged. As Ian Johnston and Rob McAuley wrote in *The Battleships*: "If ever there was an example of a 'battleship' that became a symbol of national pride, it is surely HMS *Victory*—still in commission in the Royal Navy, beautifully preserved and restored, she is the ultimate example of the power and majesty of a line-of-battle ship of 100 guns—an eighteenth century ancestor of the great battleships that were to follow."

Nelson's body was returned to England for his state funeral. He has become known as one of Britain's great heroes and has been the subject of many monuments throughout the country, the most impressive being Nelson's Column in Trafalgar Square, London.

Ship-of-the-line evolution progressed dramatically later in the nineteenth century with the coming of steam propulsion power as a part of the industrial revolution. This development led to the earliest metal-hulled warships, and that of the new projectile shells which could breach the wooden hulls of the contemporary warships, which exposed the need for iron-clad hulls. That, in turn, led to the development of stronger, more protective iron hulls, as well as more powerful projectiles or shells that could breach the new iron hulls.

The performance enhancement provided by steam power, together with a new type of screw propeller, led to a wholly new and innovative type of battleship, an example of which being the French *Gloire* class. *Gloire*, at the head of a four-ship class of battleships, while still being rigged for sail, was able to achieve a thirteen-knot speed. She displaced 5,630 tons, was 255 feet long with a fifty-six-foot beam and a twenty-eight-foot draught and was armed with thirty-six 6.4-inch muzzle-loading guns spaced along both sides of her decks. Her iron armour belt was 4.7 inches thick. The French had planned on building as many as thirty *Gloire*-class battleships, but were prevented from achieving that goal by their limited iron-making capacity. In fact, only *Couronne*, of the first four ships of the class, was made with an all-iron hull.

At that time, iron-clad battleship construction in Britain was proceeding impressively, with two important examples being *Black Prince* and *Warrior*. They had both been completed by 1862 and their superior technology enabled them to outperform the vessels of the *Gloire* class and regain battleship prestige for Britain. The iron-hulled *Warrior*, in particular, was faster and far better armed than the French battleships. Her pioneering design incorporated a variety of new and creative features including forced-air ventilation to eliminate smoke on the gundeck. She also boasted a blast-furnace in the boiler room for producing molten iron to make hollow shot. The 420-foot-long *Warrior* had a fifty-eight-foot beam, a 26-foot draught, and a 9,137-ton displacement. She was armed with ten 110-pounder guns, four 70-pounders and twenty-six 68-pounders. She was manned by a crew of 700.

Today the beautifully restored *Warrior* is on display near *Victory* in Portsmouth Naval Dockyard.

The next significant event in the history of the battleship came with the American Civil War in 1861 with the construction of a new, turret-gunned vessel for the U.S. Navy, designed to go up against the Confederates States' floating gun battery, the CSS *Virginia*, which had formerly been the frigate *Merrimac*. The *Virginia* had eight nine-inch guns in armoured gunports, and two seven-inch rifled-shell guns. American naval architect John Ericsson was commissioned to design a new gunboat to deal with the *Virginia*. The *Monitor* would be steam-powered and a raft-like design armed with a rotating twenty-foot diameter turret which mounted two eleven-inch smooth-bore guns.

In the enormous natural harbour area of Virginia known as Hampton Roads, near the entrance to Chesapeake Bay, two United States Navy frigates were attacked and sunk by the CSS *Virginia* on 8 March 1862. The following day, *Monitor* found and engaged *Virginia* and a three-hour gun battle ensued. In the action, neither ship was able to breach the armour of the other. What the action did appear to prove was that in such an engagement of new and radically different warship types, relative to the standards of the day, the sort of heavy armour they had was largely impenetrable, and that the turret-mounted guns of one made it conspicuosly overmatched against the fixed guns of the other. The relative invulnerability provided by their armour plating established the need to develop more powerful guns and the shells. It was clear too, that, while both warships had been designed for and were effective weapons for use in rather calm coastal waters, a design of somewhat different capability would be required for naval warfare on the high seas. As the century came to a close, the ability to produce steel as a replacement for the iron previously used in the construction of warships ushered in a new era in battleship design. The age of sail was almost entirely over by the dawn of the twentieth century and the burgeoning navies of the United States, Britain, Germany, Russia, and Japan were all in the process of building strong, steam-powered navies around their own versions of mammoth new battleships.

The Dreadnoughts

As the twentieth century opened, the field of battleship design and performance was dominated by a new and revolutionary vessel called the dreadnought. The word dreadnought became iconic and a generic reference for the new battleships that were launched in the immediate wake of the British Royal Navy's 1906 battleship *Dreadnought*. Earlier battleships of the great navies were then referred to as pre-dreadnoughts. The type was distinguished by its essentially big-gun armament which mounted an unprecedented total of heavy-calibre weapons, and its then-unique steam-powered turbine propulsion system.

The dreadnought concept came about as those great navies raced to substantially increase the hitting power and range of their battleships at the beginning of the new century. Their 1890s-era battleships, or pre-dreadnoughts, were generally armed with four twelve-inch heavy guns and between six and eighteen rapid-firing 4.7-inch and 7.5-inch guns, as well as a number of smaller calibre weapons. Their armament had long been planned within the naval warfare concept of long-distance combats which would gradually move in to closer ranges and finally to short-range, where their rapid-fire

below: HMS *Dreadnought* changed the battleship fleets of the world; top left: Admiral John 'Jacky' Fisher, RN, top centre: Admiral John Jellicoe, RN; top far right: Admiral David Beatty, RN.

weapons would be most effective. Most battleship navies were, by 1903, seriously reconsidering their heavy fire-power requirement.

It was no coincidence that, in the early 1900s, the navies of Britain, Japan, and the United States were all deeply involved in the planning and construction of the new, big-gun battleships. *Satsuma* was the name chosen by the Imperial Japanese Navy for its first dreadnought warship when her keel was laid down in May 1904. The Royal Navy's HMS *Dreadnought* followed in May 1905 when the British First Sea Lord, Vice Admiral Sir John 'Jackie' Fisher, took Britain to the forefront of the battleship revolution in authorizing the construction of an entirely new class of capital ship, the all big-gun battleship, HMS *Dreadnought*; and the dreadnought USS *Michigan* was laid down in December 1906 for the United States Navy. Fisher was determined to modernize the Royal Navy and prepare it to meet and surpass the challenge of the growing German Fleet. He set out to provide the Royal Navy with a new warship type of unprecedented capability, if possible, at a relatively low cost. Such a new purchase, at a rather higher cost would, he knew, not be well received by the British taxpayers, and the treasury would not support an expense of that sort if it were perceived as an extravagance. To meet the radical requirements placed upon *Dreadnought*, he knew he would have to make economies elsewhere, so Fisher found the economies by substantially reducing the existing British warship inventory and through the scrapping of hundreds of its vessels which he identified as being "too weak to fight and too slow to run away."

Among the 'casualties' on Fisher's list of inventory eliminations were many of the Royal Navy's cruisers, which he slashed in his firm belief that the British Navy of the future had to be built around a proliferation of submarines, destroyers, and fast-attack battleships in his quest for a leaner, meaner war fleet. Fisher saw the enormous importance of steam turbine power for the dreadnought, compared with the power supply of her predecessors, as perhaps her greatest asset, but he was no less impressed by her greatly improved armour and her heavy, long-range armament. He was utterly determined to impress the Germans, the Russians, the French and the Americans that, with *Dreadnought*,

below: HMS *Agamemnon* and bottom, HMS *Lord Nelson*, the battleships from which Admiral Fisher diverted armour plate, gun turrets and mountings, for use on *Dreadnought*.

Britannia still ruled the waves. To that end, he employed plenty of hype to show the world that the British Navy could quickly build and deploy *Dreadnought* in a powerful display of shipbuilding strength, industrial capacity, and naval invincibility. He spared no individual and no supplier in a ruthless pursuit to be first in launching, conducting sea trials, and operating the new class of battleship. In that quest, he encountered several irksome problems which demanded bold solutions, some of them highly unpopular in naval circles. One such was a delay in the production of the gun turrets for *Dreadnought*. He dealt with the problem by diverting turrets, armour plates and mountings that had been built and designated for the new battleships *Lord Nelson* and *Agamemnon*, to be installed in *Dreadnought*.

HMS *Dreadnought* was laid down in Portsmouth Shipyard in October 1905 and was launched in record time, in February 1906 for her preliminary trials, thanks in large part to the super-human efforts of the 1,100 shipyard workers there. Her entire construction time was just 366 days, with only two months more needed for her final fitting-out. When the finished, sea-worthy first example of her class appeared to the world, all other battleships suddenly fell into two distinct groups: pre-dreadnoughts and dreadnoughts.

The new dreadnoughts were immediately perceived as symbolic of great national power and presence on the seas and fostered an intense renewal of the naval arms race between the United Kingdom and Germany. The enormous emphasis placed on the dreadnoughts and their expanding technology spread across the globe and the rapid evolution of their requirements and design resulted in significant improvements in their armament, armour and propulsion technologies. That evolution led over the next five years to the development of bigger and much more powerful battleships known as super-dreadnoughts, many of which replaced the majority of the early dreadnoughts following the end of the First World War, as a result of the terms of the Washington Naval Treaty of 1922. Several of the newer super-dreadnoughts remained in active service throughout the Second World War.

As the Royal Navy planners rushed to take advantage of the new steam turbine engines for use in ocean-going warships, they were profoundly influenced by the design ideas of the naval architect Sir Charles Algernon Parsons. His Parsons Marine Steam Turbine Company had impressively demonstrated the advantages of turbine power for warships, with a turbine-driven destroyer in 1901 and a turbine-driven cruiser, the *Amethyst*, the following year. The Royal Navy Committee on Designs, appointed by the Admiralty, advised the Navy in 1905 that in future turbine power should be used exclusively in all classes of warships, with the dreadnoughts being the first battleship class to incorporate them.

Vessels of many types were then undergoing sea trials having been fitted with the new turbine engines. The Cunard passenger line had committed to fitting them in the new liners *Lusitania* and *Mauretania*. But in that early part of the new century, there actually occurred only a single example of major conflict between great dreadnought fleets—the Battle of Jutland fought on 31 May-1 June 1916, in which warships of the Royal Navy's Grand Fleet engaged those of the Imperial German Navy's High Seas Fleet, in the North Sea near Jutland, Denmark. The Grand Fleet was under the command of Admiral Sir John Jellicoe and the High Seas Fleet was commanded by Vice Admiral Reinhard Scheer, whose aim was to trap and destroy a significant number of the British warships, in order to ease the pressure placed on German merchant shipping by the Grand Fleet.

In that major sea battle of WWI, the strategy of the Royal Navy called for the Grand Fleet to pursue and engage the German fleet, to keep it away from Britain's own shipping lanes. Initially, the Germans sent the fast scouting group of Vice Admiral Franz Hipper's five battlecruisers to attract the battlecruisers of Vice Admiral Sir David Beatty into the area where the German main fleet was concentrated. But Beattys force actually arrived near Hipper's battlecruisers in the afternoon of the 31st, well before the Germans had expected them to appear. Still, the unprepared German crews rallied and managed to lure the British vessels into the presence of the main German fleet. In the action that followed, Beatty lost two from his force of six battlecruisers and four battleships. By the end of the afternoon, the German and British battle fleets, totalling nearly 250 warships, had directly engaged one another twice. A massive loss of life resulted as eleven German and fourteen British vessels were sunk. The German fleet departed in the darkness, returning to their port.

The results of Jutland included the loss of more British than German warships, and many more British sailors, but despite this, the Germans failed in their effort to destroy much of the Grand Fleet. After devoting most of that year to an unsuccessful attempt at eliminating the numerical warship advantage of the Royal Navy, the German Navy refocused its efforts on unrestricted submarine warfare and the destruction of Allied and neutral merchant shipping, which action brought the United States into the war.

HMS *Dreadnought* looked very different, and more formidable, than her predecessors. She was designed with long and clean lines and large turrets well-spaced along her ample deck. She lived up to her billing in the early sea trials. The speed and accuracy, and rate of fire, of her gunnery was pronounced excellent by her evaluators and her structure proved easily up to the strain she experienced when firing eight-gun broadsides. With a range of 6,620 nautical miles, her steam-driven quadruple-screw turbines drove her at a maximum speed of 21.6 knots and an average speed of ten knots. She was operated by a crew of up to 775 personnel. *Dreadnought* was 527 feet long, with a beam of eighty-two feet and she had eleven-inch armour on her five main turrets, each of which mounted two twelve-inch guns. In addition to her main guns, she was armed with twenty-seven twelve-pounder guns and five eighteen-inch torpedo tubes. When fully loaded, *Dreadnought* displaced 21,850 tons. As the first vessel of her class, some mistakes were made in her design and specification. The main belt armour was positioned too low, and she was equipped with anti-torpedo boat guns that were inadequate for purpose. These concerns were corrected in the subsequent British dreadnoughts.

The conversion by the Royal Navy, the U.S., and other navies to the all big-gun battleship occurred after the experience of the Russo-Japanese war of 1904 established that future naval battles would mainly be fought at long distances. The new long-range twelve-inch naval guns of the day packed massive fire power, and advances in fire control enhanced the promise of the new battleships. In the 1890s, prior to the coming of the dreadnoughts, naval battles featured smaller, medium-calibre guns, usually quick-firing six-inch types that were frequently employed over distances of between 2,000 and 4,000 yards. Naval gunnery over greater distances then was inaccurate. With good accuracy and a high rate-of-fire, these guns generated high volumes of destruction on their targets, in what was known then as 'hail of fire.'

But both British and American admirals of the time were becoming persuaded that their navies needed to be able to engage the enemy at greater distances. They were being influenced by factors such as the longer ranges of the latest model torpedoes. The light and medium naval guns at the beginning of the twentieth century had a very limited range capability and their accuracy fell off consid-

erably as the range increased. Too, their advantage of a high rate-of-fire decreased dramatically as the range demands grew.

Considerable debate continued in Britain, the United States, Russia, Japan, and elsewhere over the armament, armour, and approaches to the design of the dreadnoughts, and the 'all big-gun mixed-calibre' battleship types known as semi-dreadnoughts. In 1902 the Royal Navy debated the merits of such a design which featured four twelve-inch and twelve 9.2-inch guns. Instead, the Admiralty decided to build three additional *King Edward VII*-class mixed-gun warships. Two years later, however, it chose to return to the all big-gun idea with development of the *Lord Nelson*-class.

The concept of calibre uniformity, and the efficiencies that went with it in terms of fire control, were soon heavily influencing the dreadnought designers in Britain. The probability of high-seas battle engagements taking place at much longer ranges than in the past greatly influenced the decision to make the heaviest available guns (then twelve-inch) standard to the dreadnoughts; a decision made easier by the fact that the mounting for the newer twelve-inch guns enabled a considerably higher rate of fire, increased from a rate of one round every four minutes in 1895, to two rounds per minute in 1902.

Another important contribution to the science was that of the Italian naval architect Vittorio Cuniberti who, in a 1903 article published in *Jane's Fighting Ships*, An Ideal Battleship for the British Navy, outlined his vision of a 17,000-ton vessel with a main armament of twelve twelve-inch guns, having twelve-inch-thick armour and a top speed of twenty-eight miles per hour. He called attention to the high rate of fire of those twelve-inch guns and the rapid, concentrated firepower they could produce, to replace the old 'hail of fire' of lighter weapons previously favoured.

By the autumn of 1905, the long-time proponent of the dreadnought and the advancement of related technologies for the Royal Navy main battle fleet, First Sea Lord John Fisher, was actively promoting the 'all big-gun battleship' concept. Fisher took pride in the reputation he had gained as 'the father of Britain's great dreadnought battleship fleet'. When he came into office Fisher wanted to explore the possibilites of another new generation of battleship type, the dreadnought, as well as a new battlecruiser type, and, to that end, he established the Committee on Designs to come up with and duly consider the capabilities, performance, and specifications of such warships.

The fundamental goal of dreadnought planners in Britain and the other nations where the new type was being developed, was the creation and construction of a new warship that provided maximum firepower, speed, and protection within a realistic and reasonable context of cost and size. The dreadnought concept called for an 'all big-gun armament' as well as heavy armour placed primarily in a thick belt at the waterline and in one or more armoured decks. There was also to be provision for a secondary armament, command equipment, fire control, and protection against the torpedo threat.

To the work of the British Committee on Designs was added the chore of a detailed evaluation of the action reports from the Russo-Japanese naval battle of 27 May 1905 off the island of Tsushima near the Straits of Korea, the first major engagement between big-gun warships. After their evaluation the Committee members agreed a layout utilizing a main battery of ten twelve-inch guns and a secondary armament of twenty-two twelve-pounders. They also chose to commit *Dreadnought* to being powered by steam-driven turbine propulsion, previously untried in a large warship. The choice would make *Dreadnought* capable of a twenty-four mph top speed, on a somewhat smaller and less costly frame than would have been required had conventional reciprocating engines been employed. Exceptionally rapid construction followed and the new *Dreadnought*, the first in her class, was completed in early October 1906.

HMS *Dreadnought*

In the United States, meanwhile, the planning for the first two examples of the American dreadnoughts, the *South Carolina* class of warships, was completed by November 1905. Their keels were laid down in December 1906.

HMS *Dreadnought* was truly imposing, being bigger than any earlier battleship. Her appearance made all other existing battleships second rate. But John Fisher had more ideas to be explored, principally that of a new armoured battlecruiser. He intended it to carry 9.2-inch guns, but after further consideration he decided that it should be armed with twelve-inch guns. His specifications called for a vessel capable of a twenty-five knot top speed, which dictated the use of a larger hull than that of *Dreadnought*. That, combined with the great weight of the big guns, left a need to somehow conserve weight elsewhere, and he opted for the use of the ordinary light armour of conventional armoured cruisers. The first ship of the new battlecruiser class was HMS *Invincible* and she was soon to be followed down the ways by her sister ships *Indomitable* and *Inflexible*, all three of their keels being laid down in 1906 and all were completed in 1908. These first battlecruisers of *Invincible* class were steam turbine powered like *Dreadnought* and all met the twenty-five knot speed requirement. They were armed with four main turrets, each mounting two twelve-inch guns; their overall armour protection was minimal to keep the weight down. Their secondary armament consisted of sixteen four-inch guns and five eighteen-inch torpedo tubes. The *Invincible* class battlecruisers were 567 feet long and displaced 17,370 tons. Each was manned by a crew of 780.

Over the course of its career at the forefront of the world's greatest navies, the dreadnought appeared with a uniform main battery layout of its heavy guns. Variation occurred from navy to navy, with the number, arrangement, and size of the big guns specified and employed in various distinctive approaches. The original example, HMS *Dreadnought*, mounted ten twelve-inch guns. Generally, the battleships of the pre-dreadnought era employed twelve-inch guns and most of the major dreadnought-using navies retained twelve-inch gun armament. However, the Imperial German Navy chose to carry eleven-inch guns in its first dreadnought class.

Despite the commitment to all big-gun armament layouts for the dreadnought battleships in their first generation and beyond, the dreadnoughts also required a secondary level of armament for their protection from attack by enemy torpedo boats. And, following the First World War, it became essential for the battleships of these navies to be mounted with a considerable amount of light guns for anti-aircraft armament. Finally, in what was probably a hang-over from the days of the line-of-battle naval tactic, many dreadnoughts were mounted with a number of torpedo tubes in order to be able to launch a volley of torpedoes against enemy vessels steaming on a parallel course to the dreadnought(s).

The layout of the gun turrets on each dreadnought significantly affected its success achieved in combat. The British dreadnoughts, for example, were designed to carry five main gun turrets: one forward and two aft positioned on the centreline of the ship, and a further two in the 'wings' adjoining the superstructure. The layout made it possible for the crews of three turrets to shoot ahead and four on the broadside. The German dreadnoughts were designed with a main turret forward, another aft, and four more on the wings, enabling the same number of guns to fire ahead or broadside as could the British dreadnoughts. There was much experimentation in armament layout of the dreadnoughts. One example, the British *Neptune* class, had its wing turrets staggered in such a way as to allow all ten of its main guns to fire broadside. This layout, though, came with an increased risk of blast damage to the areas of the ship over which the guns were fired. It also put the ship's frame under considerable ad-

HMS *Dreadnought*

ditional stress. *Dreadnought* designers discovered that, in placing all the main gun turrets on the centreline of the ship, the stresses on the ship's frame incurred when firing were minimized. It also enabled the entire main battery to be fired on the broadside. The downside of this layout required the hull to be somewhat longer, as well as needing additional armour and thus added weight. The placement of the ammunition magazines serving each turret then compromised the positioning and distribution of the ship's engines and boilers.

The ultimate solution came in the form of the superfiring layout adopted by most of the world's dreadnoughts. The layout required positioning the turrets on the centreline and raising one or two, which allowed them to fire over a turret immediately forward or astern. The layout was not without concerns initially. It was feared that the blast of the raised guns would damage the lower turret, and concern that raising some turrets would raise the centre of gravity of the ship and might reduce its stability. Still, most dreadnought planners tended to accept that the superfiring layout offered the best and most efficient use of the ship's firepower from a fixed number of guns, and the layout was eventually adopted by most of them. By the time of the Second World War, the superfiring layout was standard on battleships.

In the developmental years of the dreadnought battleships, all main turrets mounted two guns. In time, however, some dreadnought designers turned to turret installations which mounted three or even four big guns, allowing the hull to be shorter and providing more options for the interior layout of the vessel. This advantage had to be weighed against the risk of a turret being destroyed by an enemy shell and the resultant higher loss of main armament. There was additional risk that blast waves from each gun barrel would interfere with the other guns in the turret, reducing the rate of fire for the turret. Ultimately, most navies adopted three-gun turrets on their battleships. Some, including the Royal Navy, in the *King George V* class, and the French Navy, in the *Richelieu* class, opted for four-gun turret installations.

A further development in the race to increase the power of battleship armament in the age of the dreadnought came through experimentation with larger calibre guns firing heavier shells, and longer gun barrels which increased the muzzle velocity, the range and penetration capability of the weapon. A side effect of increased muzzle velocity, however, was increased barrel wear, leading to decreasing accuracy and more frequent barrel replacement. In 1910, that disadvantage made the United States Navy give serious consideration to eliminating practice firing by the crews of its battleship big guns. A further disadvantage of the heavier guns was that, in addition to weighing more, their heavier, slower shells had to be fired at a higher angle to achieve the same range, which affected the design of the turrets. On the plus side, those heavier shells created less air resistance, which increased their penetrating power over a long range.

In another developmental step, just after the end of the First World War, both Japan and the United States designed and laid down the keels for their new *Nagato* and *Colorado* class battleships respectively, which mounted sixteen-inch guns. And both Japan and the United Kingdom had plans under way for new battleships carrying eighteen-inch guns, but the restrictions imposed by the Washington Naval Treaty conference of 1922 quashed those plans.

Through the period leading to the First World War, the war itself and the early aftermath, the dreadnought and battlecruiser designers of the great naval powers struggled to produce warships of ever greater speed, firepower, and protection, which increased displacement, size and overall cost. In the

1922 Washington Naval Treaty, a limit of 35,000 tons was imposed on the displacement of capital ships and in the years immediately after the Washington Treaty conference, several new battleships were designed and commissioned which came up to that new limit. But the limit became irrelevent in the 1930s when Japan elected to leave the restraints of the treaty. When she left the treaty, Japan immediately broke the limitations on new battleship design and construction by implementing her *Yamato* class in 1937, a warship mounting 18.1-inch guns. They even had plans to build a *Super Yamato* class warship mounting twenty-inch guns. The Germans were also in the preliminary conceptual design stage on battleships mounting twenty-inch guns and there is evidence that the German chancellor Hitler wanted the development of a mammoth twenty-four-inch gun for a new class of German battleship. But these concepts went no further than preliminary work.

In action, the early dreadnoughts were tactically disposed to pitched battle encounters with other battleships. Such encounters generally took place at ranges of up to 10,000 yards. The shells would tend to take relatively flat trajectories, causing them to hit the target vessel at or near the waterline, causing primary damage to the most vital aspects of the target. Because of this, the bulk of early dreadnought armour was a thick, eleven-inch belt, positioned to protect the warship's engineering spaces, which were further protected by the ship's coal bunkers. Thinner layers of steel armour were employed on the decks of the dreadnought to protect her innards from shell fragments detonated on the superstructure.

Finally, in a protection scheme for the early dreadnoughts, the hull was subdivided below the waterline into many watertight compartments. If the ship's hull should be holed by torpedo, shell, mine, or collision, theoretically at least, just one compartmentalized area would be flooded and the dreadnought would survive the strike. This method of protection was enhanced by eliminating the provision of any doors between the various underwater compartments. The system was, however, not perfect and, in practice, some flooding did occur and spread between the underwater compartments. A further advance in this area of protection for the vessel came with the addition of an inner bulkhead along the side of the hull, which was separated from the outer hull by one or more compartments which were normally filled with fuel oil, coal, or water. This inner bulkhead was lightly armoured to take splinters in an explosion.

As the British and the other great navies of the world were expanding their fleets and adding dreadnoughts to them in considerable numbers, the British government became concerned about the rate of Germany's rapidly growing warship inventory. Britain had thus far been calm about her dreadnought force and its capability to outgun and outperform the other major naval powers. That situation prevailed until 1908, when a Liberal British government cut the Navy's budgetary allocation for new battleships. The action brought on a heated parliamentary debate over the nation's strategic priorities and defence needs and their costs. Meanwhile, two new British battleships then under construction were cancelled, just as the British Admiralty learned that the Germans were increasing their battleship building programme. The British admirals realized that Germany would catch up with Britain in battleship numbers within the next three years. For nearly a year the debate raged until, in the summer of 1909, agreement was reached on the authorization of construction for four new dreadnoughts, to be followed in 1910 with authorization for building four more, should the Germans maintain their battleship building programme at the same pace.

In that nervous time, the Commonwealth nations of Australia and New Zealand showed their concern about the German naval threat by offering to pay for the construction of two new British battlecruisers, the *Australia* and the *New Zealand*. And as Britain and Germany approached the start of the First World War, the British had built thirty-two new battleships and ten battlecruisers, while the Germans had built nineteen new battleships and six battlecruisers.

In the First World War, HMS *Dreadnought* did not really live up to her billing, and in her entire history she managed to sink just one enemy warship, a German submarine which she tracked down and rammed. Indeed, the whole of the British dreadnought fleet began to require substantial maintenance and refitting in home ports after only two months service in WWI. At any point in the war, the British Navy had to cope without the availability of two-to-three dreadnoughts.

The rise of the German U-boat threat to the battleship was underscored late in 1914 by a number of successful torpedo strikes on British cruisers. Mines were another scurge of the Allied conventional warships, an example being the destruction of the newly-commissioned superdreadnought HMS *Audacious*, which struck and was sunk by such a weapon. Paranoia was growing in the British Navy about the vulnerability of battleships.

As usually happens at the end of a major conflict, the populations of the warring nations want only to forget everything about the tragic events, including the losses, the misery wrought, and the financial costs imposed. Britain, for example, entered a major programme to scrap many of her warships including HMS *Dreadnought*. She would be remembered though, not for her performance in WWI, but for the influence she spread through the world's navies which affected their capital ship planning and construction.

Struggling to bring an end to the crippling financial programmes of the war and the massive arms race to date, the main naval powers sat in conference to negotiate the Washington Naval Treaty of 1922. Therein, lists were developed of warships, which included the majority of the older dreadnoughts as well as most of the newer warships then under construction—that were directed to be scrapped or put out of use. Those vessels that survived the treaty lists, including the newest of the superdreadnoughts, became the foundation of world capital ship strength through the 1930s and into the Second World War.

Bigger than any existing battleship, the appearance of *Dreadnought* made all other battleships obsolete. *Dreadnought* looked different, more formidable than her predecessors. The new dreadnoughts were immediately perceived as symbolic of great national power and presence on the seas and fostered an intense renewal of the naval arms race between Britain and Germany.

Jutland

A key advantage of the British Royal Navy from the onset of the First World War in 1914, was the ability to intercept and read German naval messages. This proved of particular interest to the Admiralty when, in mid-May 1916, it discovered that a number of U-boats had departed their normal station positions on the Atlantic trade routes, and on 29 May, when the German naval messages contained the information that the German High Seas Fleet had been ordered to readiness for action on 31 May.

On that day the battlecruiser group of German Admiral Franz von Hipper was ordered from its North Sea bases. The order came from Vizeadmiral Reinhard Scheer, German High Seas Fleet commander, and the mission of Hipper's vessels was to snare the British Grand Fleet, or as much of it as he could lure from harbour. The plan called for his warships to tease the battlecruisers of the British Navy out to intercept his force comprised of five battlecruisers, twenty-two battleships, eleven cruisers, six pre-dreadnoughts, and sixty-one torpedo boats. The role of the German U-boats in the affair was mining the British routes from the Royal Navy facilities at Rosyth, Cromarty, and Scapa Flow. Thereafter, the U-boats were to hide near those British bases, ready to torpedo the British dreadnoughts on their way out of harbour. Finally, it was the assignment of the U-boat captains involved to report all enemy warship movements to Scheer. Further reconnaissance was to come from German Zeppelin airships as to the size, disposition and movement of the enemy force.

British Admiral Sir David Beatty commanded a force of battlecruisers had that departed the harbour at Rosyth on a mission to scout the area near Skagerrak Strait, before heading on to a position within seventy miles of the British Grand Fleet and then proceeding south from Scapa Flow. The Fleet was commanded then by Admiral John Jellicoe who was under orders to take it to a point approximately 100 miles east of Aberdeen. It was his assignment to report all ship movements of the coming action with the German warships, to the Operations Room of the Admiralty, which would be running the battle from London. In his flagship, the battleship *Iron Duke*, Jellicoe led the Grand Fleet out of Scapa Flow late in the evening of 30 May and had it on station the following afternoon.

Almost as soon as Beatty's battlecruisers departed Rosyth, Admiral Scheer's plan began to crumble. His force of submarines somehow failed to effectively attack the British warships steaming from Scapa, and the weather simultaneously deteriorated, preventing the German Zeppelins from operating. As the afternoon wore on, the airships were able to fly their recces, but to little avail as the visibility then was minimal. Scheer was left with almost no useful information about the movements of the British warships. He had no idea that the entire British fleet was steaming directly towards his High Seas Fleet. Intelligence failure was not confined to the German side, by any means. Someone in the Admiralty Operations Room evidently misinterpreted a German naval message they had intercepted in London and, as a result, sent a signal to Jellicoe at noon that the *Friedrich der Grosse*, flagship of Admiral Scheer, had not yet left its Jade River moorings near Wilhelmshaven. Thus, both of the opposing fleet commanders were hopelessly ignorant that the other was rapidly approaching.

The meeting of the two massive, powerful fleets was now inevitable. And, in another strange turn of events, some cruisers of both sides were sent off to investigate smoke on the horizon which was, in fact, only a Danish steamer. But the opposing cruisers sighted their opposite numbers at a closing distance of about fourteen miles and turned to close that range. Both sides at that point thought

below: Battlecruisers of the German High Seas Fleet; bottom left: Demise of the British battlecruiser *Queen Mary*; *bottom right:* HMS *Valiant*, circa 1932, in the Cromarty Firth.

above: HMS *Valiant*; below:
HMS *Malaya* leaving New
York harbour after completion
of repairs at Brooklyn Navy
Yard in July 1941.

they were luring the opposition into a trap. As the range narrowed, the British cruisers *Phaeton* and *Galatea* opened fire on the German cruiser *Elbing*, which responded with its own guns. *Galatea* signalled Beatty of the German's position and Beatty altered the course of his warships. By now weather and reconnaissance conditions had got worse. An hour later, however, crewmen aboard the German battlecruisers spotted the smoke columns of the British fleet. Their sighting coincided with Beatty learning that his men had just sighted some of the German ships. He responded by leading six of his battlecruisers into a fight with five German battlecruisers. In his rush to battle, Beatty lacked the key fact that Admiral Scheer's entire High Seas Fleet was at that moment bearing down on his force. As Beatty's ships approached those of Hipper, Beatty ordered a course change in order to position his battlecruisers between Hipper's and the German bases. Hipper, meanwhile, was attempting to draw Beatty's ships towards the German main force which was then only fifty miles away. At that point, neither Hipper nor Scheer realized that Jellicoe's main British force was rapidly closing on them.

Haze, smoke and generally poor visibility maintained through the afternoon, as did relatively calm sea. With their backs to the sun, the German warship crews had an advantage with the British ships better illuminated and their own vessels somewhat harder to see. When the big gunfire began, the added smoke mixed with the haze layer to further reduce visibility in the combat area.

Organizationally, the *Lutzow*, flagship of German Admiral Hipper, was in the lead of his battlecruisers, *Derfflinger*, *Seydlitz*, *Moltke*, and *Von der Tann*. Beatty's own flagship, *Lion*, led the British battlecruisers *Queen Mary*, *Tiger*, *Princess Royal*, *New Zealand*, and *Indefatigable*. When the gunners of *Lutzow* opened fire *Lion* was hit immediately, her magazines flooded, a turret struck and its entire crew killed, and fierce fires were burning all over the ship. In the late afternoon, it was apparent that the British battlecruisers were getting the worst of the action and the German equivalents were getting off rather lightly. *Indefatigable* suffered in the extreme as three eleven-inch shells from the guns of *Derfflinger* fell on her aft starboard quarter. Burning furiously, the British ship then received another large shell in her forward gun turret, followed shortly by another. Seconds later the great warship blew up in an enormous orange fireball and sank quickly by the stern, rolling as she went down at 4:03 p.m. There were only two survivors of the crew.

Then, at 4:25, the *Derfflinger* gunners targetted the battlecruiser *Queen Mary*, hitting her in such a way as to create a massive explosion. HMS *Tiger*, the next ship in the line after *Queen Mary*, was forced to swerve heavily in an effort to dodge the wreck of *Queen Mary*, which was now being fired on by *Seydlitz* too. The shells of *Seydlitz* tore into *Mary*'s magazines, causing an explosion so ferocious as to blow the ship in two. An officer of HMS *Tiger* recalled: "The *Queen Mary* was next ahead of us, and I remember watching her for a little, and saw one salvo straddle her. Three shells out of four hit, and the impression one got of seeing the splinters fly and the dull red burst was as if no damage had been done, but that the armour was keeping the shell out. The next salvo that I saw straddled her, and two more shells hit her. As they hit I saw a dull red glow amidships and then the ship seemed to open out like puff ball, or one of those toadstool things when one squeezes it. Then there was another dull red glow somewhere forward, and the whole ship seemed to collapse inwards. The funnels and masts fell into the middle, and the hull was blown outwards. The roofs of the turrets were blown a hundred feet high, then everything was smoke, and a bit of the stern was the only part of the ship left above the water. The *Tiger* put her helm hard-a-starboard and we just cleared the remains of the *Queen Mary*'s stern by a few feet."

A survivor of the *Queen Mary* crew, Petty Officer E. Francis, remembered: ". . . I clambered up over the slimy bilge keel and fell off into the water, followed, I should think, by about five other men. I struck away from the ship as hard as I could, and must have covered nearly fifty yards, when there was a big smash, and, stopping and looking round, the air seemed to be full of fragments and flying pieces. A large piece seemed to be right above my head and, acting on impulse, I dipped under to avoid being struck, and stayed under as long as I could. I then came up again and, coming behind me I heard a rush of water and realized it was the suction or backwash from the ship which had just gone down. I hardly had time to fill my lungs with air when it was on me. I felt there was no use struggling against it so I let myself go for a moment or two, and then struck out, but I thought it was a losing game and thought 'What's the use of struggling? I'm done.' I then started afresh and something bumped against me. I grasped it and found it was a large hammock, which pulled me to the surface, more dead than alive. I rested on it, but felt I was getting very weak. I roused myself enough to look around for something more substantial to support me. Floating right in front of me was a piece of timber. I managed to push myself on the hammock, closer to the timber and grasped a piece of rope hanging over the side. My next difficulty was to get on top. I managed to get my arms through a strop, and then I must have become unconscious."

The *Queen Mary* sank with the loss of 1,285 men. Only nine of her crew survived. Hurrying to the rescue now were four *Queen Elizabeth* class battleships, *Barham*, *Malaya*, *Valiant*, and *Warspite*, all armed with fifteen-inch guns capable of hitting targets at a range of 19,000 yards. The German ships targetted by these rapidly advancing Royal Navy vessels could not respond from such a distance and were forced to simply zig-zag in the encounter. *Barham*'s gun crews took aim at *Von der Tann*, as *Valiant* took on *Moltke*. Beatty, meanwhile, was trying to buy some time as he awaited the engagement of the entire Grand Fleet. He ordered his destroyers to launch a torpedo attack. In the attack, a British torpedo tore a great hole in the side of *Seydlitz*, heavily damaging her. She held her position, however, among her sister battlecruisers.

Soon, the battleships of the German High Seas Fleet appeared on the horizon and Beatty signalled Jellicoe, who ordered a feint maneuver in an attempt to lure the German warships into proximity with the Grand Fleet. The trick failed and as the four British battleships slowly turned to improve their positions relative to the enemy vessels, German shells rained down on *Malaya* and *Barham*, causing many casualties. The British battleships were returning fire on the Germans, scoring several hits on the battleships *Grosser Kurfürst* and *Markgraf*.

Now the battlecruisers of Admiral Beatty were heading north to join with the ships of the Grand Fleet. Admiral Jellicoe ordered Rear Admiral Horace Hood to take three *Invincible* class battlecruisers ahead, to the assistance of Beatty. On the German side, Admiral Hipper's warships were in the lead of the whole High Seas Fleet, chasing Beatty's force and plunging headlong towards the Grand Fleet.

Beatty elected to turn his battlecruisers around to re-engage Hipper's ships at just before 5:30. In so doing, the British vessels now achieved the lighting advantage and made good use of it. As the two forces closed on each other, all began firing and, in just minutes, *Von der Tann* lost the use of all her big guns. *Seydlitz* was fighting a major fire, *Lutzow* was badly damaged and, having suffered heavy damage to her bow, *Derfflinger* was taking on water. As the situation deteriorated for Hipper, he decided to bring up his destroyers to attack the British line. Horace Hood's three battlecruisers arrived at that point, and set out to scatter the German destroyers.

If ever in the Battle of Jutland, top-quality intelligence gathered through fresh, thorough reconnaissance was needed by both the British and Germans, it was now. But it did not exist for either side.

below"The German battlecruiser SMS *Von der Tann*; bottom: SMS *Derfflinger*, raised from Scapa Flow where she was scuttled in June 1919. *Derfflinger*, together with SMS *Seydlitz*, destroyed HMS *Queen Mary* in the Battle of Jutland.

far left: Admiral Reinhard Scheer; centre left: Admiral Franz von Hipper; lower left and right: The heavily damaged German battlecruiser SMS *Seydlitz* after the Battle of Jutland; below: HMS *Queen Mary*.

Visibility from the bridge of *Iron Duke* at that moment was less than seven miles and Jellicoe was unaware of the current position, speed and bearing of the German fleet. He believed, though, that he probably had only a matter of minutes to re-position the ships of his Grand Fleet to bring all of their big guns to bear on the enemy when their ships came within range, and acted to re-form his fleet into a single column nine miles long. The move placed his newest, most capable battleships in position to open the action and, with completion of the maneuver, his ships joined up with the Grand Fleet.

The greatest assemblage of naval firepower in the world at that moment lay on the Jutland Bank near the Denmark coast. As the afternoon sunlight began fading, *König* and *Derfflinger* mounted an attack on HMS *Invincible*, the flagship of Rear Admiral Hood. *Invincible* received a huge salvo of shells in her mid-ships turret, which started a massive fire in the magazine below, followed shortly by an explosion of sufficient force to break her hull apart. The halves of her quickly sank vertically into the relatively shallow water, her bow and stern remaining above the surface like immense tombstones. Only six of her 1,032-man crew survived.

The battle now opened out to involve nearly all the warships gathered in the waters off Denmark. Admiral Jellicoe led the Grand Fleet in a move to "cross the T" of the German fleet and his big guns then wrought the full fury of the British battleship line down on the enemy warships. Scheer had been caught in Jellicoe's trap. All he could do at that point was to reverse the course of his entire force, which he accomplished that early evening with the assistance of a large smoke screen laid by his destroyers. The German fleet began to retreat.

By 7:08 p.m., however, that retreat had been cut off by Jellicoe, who had brought the vessels of the Grand Fleet round south to again cross Scheer's T. The German ships were now exposed to an even more devastating assault by the British battleships. The desperate Admiral Scheer ordered his captains: "Charge the enemy. Ram. Ships denoted are to attack without regard to consequences." It would be known as 'the death ride.' Leading it was *Derfflinger* and she soon lost both her fire control and two turrets. *Seydlitz* was hit five times and *Lutzow* was on fire. Only *Colossus* and *Marlborough* of the Grand Fleet experienced significant battle damage in this part of the action. *Colossus* took two shell strikes, and *Marlborough* was hit by a torpedo; both were able to continue the fight.

The main action of the battle went on until 8:35 p.m. After that Admiral Jellicoe declined to continue substantial night fighting, in the belief that the potential for mistakes in ship identification, as well as possible collision, were risks too great to take in the darkness. But the pressures on Admiral Scheer were such that he felt compelled to take those risks in the hope of still being able to get his big fleet safely back to Wilhelmshaven. This he managed, but in the effort he lost the pre-dreadnought *Pommern*, destroyed when hit by a British torpedo, and *Lutzow*, which had to be sunk by German destroyers when she could no longer make steam.

The Battle of Jutland was essentially fought to an even conclusion. In the action, three British capital ships and three armoured cruisers were sunk by the Germans. The Germans lost one capital ship and one other battleship. After the battle, the British had possession of the "battlefield" and their Grand Fleet returned to its bases largely intact. Within a day, the fleet had been rearmed, refuelled, and ready for sea again.

In overall losses of men and ships, the Germans lost eleven warships; the British fourteen. In personnel, the British 6,097 men; the Germans 2,551. In strategic results, the British Grand Fleet retained their rule of the North Sea and maintained their blockade of Germany. In technology, the Germans had the edge. The shells of their big guns were filled with desensitized TNT (trinitrotoluene), an im-

top and bottom: HMS *Iron Duke*, flagship of Admiral John Jellicoe in the lead of the British Grand Fleet at the Battle of Jutland.

provement over the Lyddite-filled shells used by the British. Both sides suffered considerably from a poor quality of intelligence and inadequate communications.

The overall results of Jutland were certainly mixed. The massive arms race and the cost of it to both sides did not bring the results that either had expected. The British, who had hoped and planned for a decisive defeat of the German enemy, failed to achieve it and would not have another opportunity to beat them in a major fleet action. For their part, the Germans had to accept that their vaunted High Seas Fleet was thenceforth a coastal defence force which would basically play second fiddle to Germany's far more effective U-boats.

With the Versailles Treaty at the end of the war, the German fleet was interned, first in the Firth of Forth, Scotland, and later, in Scapa Flow, the Orkneys, where they lay at anchor, cared for by German skeleton crews who were overseen by British armed guards. As the Armistice was about to expire on 21 June 1919 when the Treaty of Versailles officially came into effect, the German Vizeadmiral Ludwig von Reuter ordered those skeleton crews to scuttle their ships, which they did. In the next twenty years, though, many of those former German warships were raised from their resting places in Scapa and towed to various breaker's yards in Britain where they were broken up for scrap. Of the great German battleships, the three sister ships, *König*, *Kronprinz*, and *Markgraf* remain on the bottom of Scapa Flow.

SMS *König*, one of three German warships of the High Seas Fleet which remain at the bottom of Scapa Flow where they were scuttled by their caretaker crews.

World War One Battleships

The big-gun warships of the First World War represented the might and power of several great navies, the most notable being those of Britain and Germany. The action took place among a mix of vessels, pre-dreadnoughts, dreadnoughts, battleships and battlecruiser types, of various designs and varying capabilities. Some of the more prominent participants are described here in a series of profiles detailing their characteristics and brief histories.

A pre-dreadnought French Navy battleship, the *Gaulois* was built at Arsenal de Brest. She was launched 6 October 1896 and commissioned 23 October 1899. The *Charlemagne* class battleship was 386 feet long, had a beam of sixty-six feet, a draught of twenty-seven feet and displaced 10,361 tons. Her top speed was twenty-one mph and her range, at ten knots, was 4,350 miles. The ship's complement was 668 men. She was armed with four twelve-inch guns, ten 5.46-inch guns, eight 3.9-inch guns, twenty 47mm Hotchkiss guns, and four 17.7-inch torpedo tubes.

Named after the tribes that inhabited France in Roman times, *Gaulois* was the sister ship of *Charlemagne*, which was also built at Brest. In the period prior to the First World War, *Gaulois* accidentally rammed the French battleship *Bouvet*. Neither vessel was seriously damaged in the incident which occurred during exercises off Golfe-Juan. When Mount Vesuvius erupted in April 1906, *Gaulois* joined with the battleships *Iéna* and *Bouvet* in aid of the survivors in the Naples area.

With the outbreak of war in 1914, *Gaulois* and some of the older pre-dreadnoughts of the French Navy were assigned troop escort duties from North Africa to France. In September, she was sent to Tenedos Island near the Gallipoli Peninsula of Turkey, to protect against an aggressive sortie by the German battlecruiser *Goeben*, and then relieved the French pre-dreadnought *Suffren* which returned to Toulon for a refit, and then carried the flag of Rear Admiral Émile Guépratte until he returned to *Suffren* in January 1915.

Gaulois joined *Suffren* in the bombardment of Turkish forts at the mouth of the Dardenelles on 19 February. On 25 February, *Gaulois* bombarded the forts at Kum Kale and Cape Helles, but was forced to retreat when she was unable to suppress the guns of the forts. As a part of a French squadron on 2 March, she shelled targets in the Gulf of Saros at the base of the Gallipoli Peninsula, and struck again at the Turkish fortifications in the Gulf of Saros on 11 March. In a further attack on the Dardenelles targets, *Gaulois* was hit by a shell just above the waterline on the starboard bow, which opened a twenty-three foot hole causing significant flooding. Escorted by *Charlemagne*, *Gaulois* managed to reach the Rabbit Islands north of Tenedos where temporary repairs were made. Three days later, she departed for Toulon under escort by *Suffren*, but the two warships encountered a violent storm on the 27th off Cape Matapan and *Gaulois* began taking on water as her repairs weakened. With the additional assistance and escort of an armoured cruiser and three torpedo boats, she was able to make it to the Bay of Navarin for additional repairs, and finally arrived at Toulon on 16 April and underwent major repairs there.

On 27 July *Gaulois* reached the Dardenelles once again and there relieved her sister ship *St Louis*, anchoring 1,100 yards offshore. On 11 August, she bombarded a Turkish gun battery at Achi Baba, receiving return fire which started a small blaze that was quickly doused. In January 1916, she joined the pre-dreadnought *République* in covering the Allied evacuation from Gallipoli.

Returning to the Eastern Mediterranean in late November, *Gaulois* was torpedoed while off the southern coast of Greece, by the German submarine *UB-47* on 27 December 1916, though under escort at the time by a destroyer and two armed trawlers. In twenty-two minutes, the ship capsized and fourteen minutes later, she sank off Cape Maleas.

HMS *Canopus*, the lead ship of the *Canopus* class of pre-dreadnought battleships, was laid down on 4 January 1897 at the Portsmouth Dockyard and was launched on 12 October that same year. *Canopus* was named for the ancient city of Canopus in Egypt, the scene of the Battle of the Nile. Commissioned on 5 December 1899, she was 431 feet long, with a beam of seventy-four feet and a draught of twenty-six feet. She displaced 12,950 tons. *Canopus* was manned by a crew of 750. Her armament included four twelve-inch guns, twelve six-inch guns, ten twelve-pounder guns and six three-pounder guns, as well as four eighteen-inch torpedo tubes.

Canopus began service with the Royal Navy's Atlantic Fleet on 22 July 1905, followed by service with the Channel Fleet in 1906 and the Home Fleet at Portsmouth in 1907. After various assignments, culminating in a transfer to South America in 1914, she left Abrolhos Rocks on 8 October as part of a British search effort for the German squadron of Admiral Graf Maximilian von Spee, then en route from the Far East to the South Atlantic. She arrived at Stanley in the Falkland Islands on 18 October to assume guard ship and escort duties there. Unable to make more than twelve knots while a part of the cruiser squadron commanded by Rear Admiral Christopher Cradock in the hunt for the German squadron, *Canopus* was left behind when the British squadron encountered Spee's warships. In the ensuing action, much of the British force was destroyed and Cradock killed in the Battle of Coronel, 1 November 1914. Captain Heathcoat Grant, commander of *Canopus*, took the ship

back to Stanley where he positioned her near the mudflats in such a way as to enable her to defend the harbour entrance. He reduced her visibility by removing her topmasts and having her camouflaged. He also established an observation post on high ground, with a telephone link to the ship, and assigned a detachment of seventy Royal Marines with some of her twelve-pounder guns on shore in defence of Stanley. On 7 December, the battlecruiser squadron of Admiral Sir Frederic Sturdee arrived at Stanley to reinforce *Canopus*. The next morning, Grant's land-based observers spotted the smoke of Spee's vessels on the horizon and the gun crews of *Canopus* opened fire on the German warships in the first shots of the Battle of the Falklands. Shells from *Canopus* struck the armoured cruiser *Gneisenau* in the after funnel. Spee then aborted his intended attack on the British coaling station in the Falklands and fled the area. His force was pursued by Sturdee's ships which caught and destroyed the German squadron.

Canopus was transferred to the Meditarranean and the Dardenelles campaign in February 1915 and participated in the attack of 2 March on the Turkish forts there, taking hits in the return fire that ripped off her topmast and damaged her after funnel and wardroom. On 8 March she covered the shelling of the forts by HMS *Queen Elizabeth* and the efforts of British minesweepers trying to clear the mines in the area of Kephes, and followed that work with involvement in a heavy attack on the Narrows forts on 18 March.

Her next assignment was to assist the light cruiser HMS *Talbot* in escorting the damaged battlecruiser HMS *Inflexible* from Murdos to Malta, towing *Inflexible* at one point when the crippled vessel was no longer able to make steam.

Canopus later returned to the Dardenelles to take part in the blockade of Smyrna and the main landings on 25 April. Her sister ship, *Albion*, became stranded on a sandbank while under heavy fire

far left: The French Navy battleship *Gaulois* leaving Mudros Bay for the Dardenelles; below: The *Gaulois* capsizing after being torpedoed by the German U-boat *UB-47* on 27 December 1916.

below: The semi-dreadnought battleship *Radetzky* of the Austro-Hungarian Navy in 1908; right: The British pre-dreadnought *Canopus*, the lead battleship of her class of six, was commissioned in 1899.

on 22 May and *Canopus* towed her free. *Canopus* returned to the United Kingdom in April 1916 for a major refit. In February 1918 she became an accommodation ship.

Her namesake was the nineteenth century Austrian Field Marshal Joseph Radetzky von Radetz. The SMS *Radetzky* was the lead ship of the *Radetzky* class of three pre-dreadnought battleships built by Stabilimento Tecnico, Trieste, for the Austro-Hungarian Navy, that preceded the larger and more powerful *Tegetthoff* class of dreadnoughts. *Radetzky* was commissioned in January 1911, She displaced 14,700 tons, was 456 feet long, had a beam of eighty-two feet, and a draught of twenty-six feet seven inchs. With a twenty-three mph top speed, she had a 4,000-nautical mile range at twelve mph. Her complement included 890 officers and men. Her armament was comprised of four twelve-inch guns, eight 9.4-inch guns, twenty 3.9-inch rapid-fire cannon, six eleven-pounder guns and three eighteen-inch torpedo tubes.

    Radetzky conducted a number of training cruises prior to the outbreak of the First World War. In August 1914, when the German battlecruisers *Breslau* and *Goeben* were refueling in Messina, warships of the Royal Navy began assembling outside of the port there with the intention of trapping the German vessels. At that point the German Navy asked for the assistance of their Austro-Hungarian ally in the situation. Reluctance on the part of the Austro-Hungarian High Command resulted as they were hesitant to get involved in hostilities with the British. The Germans then softened their request, asking only that Austro-Hungarian fleet steam as far as Brindisi, to which it agreed, and *Radetzky* sailed with them on the proviso that the fleet actively assist the German vessels only while in Austro-Hungarian waters. In the operation, the German ships managed to successfully break out of the harbour into the Mediterranean.

In her next action, *Radetzky* came to the aid of some Austro-Hungarian Navy pre-dreadnoughts that were shelling French artillery batteries at Cattaro. On 21 October, *Radetzky* arrived in the area to bombard the French, forcing them to abandon their position.

In a part of the Austro-Hungarian campaign against the Kingdoms of Serbia and Montenegro in 1915, *Radetzky* and the Austro-Hungarian fleet left their base at Pola to bombard the naval base at Ancona. In the action, she helped to cover the cruisers and destroyers participating in the attack on Ancona and the nearby coastline. In the area they encountered two Italian destroyers which they attacked. One escaped, but the other, *Turbine*, was badly damaged in the fight. Following the action with *Turbine*, *Radetzky* shelled and destroyed a railroad bridge near Fermo, hindering troop and supply movements in the area. When Italian warships from bases at Taranto and Brindisi arrived to deal with them, the Austro-Hungarian ships had already returned to Pola.

The campaign attack by the Austro-Hungarian ships was meant to delay the Italian Army deploying its men and equipment along the Austro-Hungarian border by destroying critical transportation systems. It proved highly successful for the attackers.

Thereafter in the war, a shortage of coal to fuel the warships of the Austro-Hungarian Navy caused the diversion of the remaining coal to the newer *Tegetthoff* class of battleships. This led to a reduced use of *Radetzky* and the ships of her class in favour of a new emphasis on the use of submarines and mines.

After a strange sequence of events near the end of the war in 1918, *Radetzky* was ceded to the Italian Navy. She was broken up in Italy in 1920.

Named for the Prussian province of Hannover, the SMS *Hannover* was the second of five *Deutschland* class pre-dreadnoughts built for the German Imperial Navy. Launched in September 1905 and commissioned in October 1907, *Hannover* was, practically, an obsolete capital ship even before she was completed, as that event came more than twelve months after the commissioning of the wholly revolutionary HMS *Dreadnought*, a faster and more powerful big-gun battleship.

The 13,200-ton *Hannover* was 419 feet long, with a beam of seventy-three feet and a draught of just under twenty-seven feet. Her top speed was slightly more than twenty mph and her range was 4,800 nautical miles at ten knots. Her complement was made up of thirty-five officers and 708 men. Her armament consisted of four eleven-inch guns, fourteen 6.7-inch guns, twenty-two 3.5-inch guns, and six eighteen-inch torpedo tubes.

Hannover was assigned to guard the Altenbruch roadstead at the mouth of the Elbe River in northern Germany when the First World War began. The German Imperial Navy was then busy readying its fleet for action and improving the armour of many of its vessels through modifications made at Kiel. In mid-December, the fleet was to send its great battlecruisers to bombard the English coast at Whitby, Scarborough and Hartlepool. What might have been one of the mightiest big-gun encounters in history was averted at the last moment. Twelve German dreadnoughts and eight pre-dreadnoughts had steamed to within twelve miles of a squadron of six British battleships. As the destroyer screens of both sides began to engage, the overall German commander, Admiral Friedrich von Ingenohl, mistakenly concluded that his force was facing the entire British Grand Fleet, and elected to break off the developing encounter and take his force back to Germany.

On 24 January 1915, *Hannover* was acting in support of some threatened German battlecruisers in the Battle of Dogger Bank, and on 17 April she was supporting a minelaying operation near the Swarte Bank. She underwent major refitting in Kiel through July before participating in more minelaying operations. In April 1916 she sailed with the German fleet to bombard Lowestoft and Yarmouth, but visibility deteriorated and the operation was called off before the elements of the lurking British fleet could gain an advantage. The operation was remounted in late May and this time *Hannover* was positioned at the rear of the German line. As the German warships steamed north, they were ordered in a high-speed pursuit of the retreating battleships of British V Battle Squadron. In the chase, *Hannover* and her pre-dreadnought sister ships were left far behind by the faster German dreadnoughts. By 19:30 that evening, virtually the entire British Grand Fleet had arrived in the area of the German fleet, and its commander, Admiral Reinhard Scheer, had to act quickly and cope with the handicap of having a force comprising several of the relatively slow *Deutschland* class pre-dreadnoughts. Those ships, having fallen behind the main German big-gun force, now threatened the commander's chances of turning his entire force onto a new, more advantageous course. Rear Admiral Franz Mauve, in command of the slower, pre-dreadnought force, considered moving his ships to the rear of the line, just astern of the main force dreadnoughts, but believed that in so doing, his ships would interfere with the maneuvering of Admiral Franz von Hipper's battlecruisers, and chose instead to attempt to reposition his pre-dreadnoughts at the front of the line. The Battle of Jutland was under way. *Hannover* would survive the battle unscathed and would return to picket duty in the mouth of the Elbe where her career had begun. She later served in various capacities mainly in German waters, until 1936 when she was finally struck from the naval register. In May 1944 the process of breaking her up began at Bremerhaven.

Before the start of the First World War, the British Royal Navy pre-dreadnought HMS *Britannia*, to

below left: Gunnery shipmates of HMS Britannia in 1912; below right: The sinking of Britannia on 9 November 1918; bottom: The *Helgoland* class battleship SMS *Ostfriesland* of the Imperial German Navy circa 1911.

gether with her sister ships of the *King Edward VII* class, *Africa*, *Commonwealth*, *Dominion*, *Hibernia*, *Hindustan*, *King Edward VII*, and *Zealandia*, were formed into the Third Battle Squadon of the Home Fleet, which was then detached to the Mediterranean in November 1912. The squadron took part in a blockade of Montenegro and the occupation of Scutari during the First Balkan War. With the beginning of the First World War, *Britannia* and the squadron were assigned to the Grand Fleet and based at Rosyth.

Laid down in February 1902 and launched on 10 December 1904, *Britannia* was 453 feet long, with a beam of seventy-eight feet and a draught of twenty-six feet nine inches. She displaced 16,350 tons, had a top speed of twenty-one mph, and a range of 5,270 nautical miles at ten knots. Her complement was 777 and her armament consisted of four twelve-inch guns, four 9.2-inch guns, ten six-inch guns, fourteen twelve-pounder guns, fourteen three-pounder guns, and five eighteen-inch torpedo tubes.

Ingloriously, *Britannia* was run aground on 26 January 1915 and suffered considerable damage to the bottom of her hull. It took thirty-six hours to refloat her and three months to repair her in Devonport Dockyard. When she returned to fleet service in April, *Britannia* and her sisters were tasked with steaming at the heads of the divisions of the superior dreadnoughts, acting as protection against enemy mines and, occasionally, being the first to encounter them.

Following two refits in 1917, *Britannia* returned to action and, near the end of the war, on 9 November 1918, she was steaming near the entrance to the Strait of Gibraltar when she was struck by a torpedo fired by the German submarine *UB-50*, off Cape Trafalgar. While listing ten degrees moments after the explosion, a second explosion started a fire in one of her magazines, which in turn caused yet another explosion. With her inner spaces in darkness through lack of power, her crew struggled to locate the flooding valves of the magazines in order to open them to properly flood the burning magazines. For more than two and a half hours, *Britannia* remained in her ten-degree list, giving most of the crew time to safely abandon her. Most of the fifty crewmen who died in the action were lost to toxic smoke from the burning cordite in the magazines. Eighty crewmen were injured, while thirty-nine officers and 673 men were saved. Two days later, the Armistice ending the war was signed. *Britannia* was the last warship of the Royal Navy to be lost in the First World War.

The *New York* class battleship USS *Texas*, BB-35, named in honour of the state of Texas, is the second warship of the United States Navy to carry that name. Laid down on 17 April 1911 and launched 18 May 1912, the *Texas* was 573 feet long, with a beam of ninety-five feet and a draught of just under twenty-eight feet. Capable of a top speed of twenty-four mph, she displaced 27,000 tons. Her armament consisted of ten fourteen-inch guns, twenty-one five-inch guns, four three-pounder guns, and four twenty-one-inch torpedo tubes. After various modifications, by 1945 her displacement had increased to 33,000 tons.

While a part of the American Atlantic fleet in the time of the First World War, *Texas* alternated between a training schedule off the Virginia Capes, and gunnery and tactical exercises in the Caribbean, both activities lasting for about two years, until February 1917 when unrestricted submarine warfare led to the United States entering the war against Germany. Assigned to continue her battle exercises in the area of the Virginia Capes and Hampton Roads through mid-August, *Texas* then began training gun crews to serve aboard merchant vessels such as the *Mongolia*. On 19 April a *Texas*-trained gun crew aboard *Mongolia* spotted a surfaced German submarine and opened fire on it, the first Amer-

below: The USS *Texas*
transitting the Gatun
Locks of the Panama
Canal in June 1937.

below: Sailors from the crew of the USS *Texas* in 1918.

ican shots fired in the war.

After a period of refitting in the New York Navy Yard, *Texas* became grounded at Block Island, New York, when the crew made an erroneous turn in trying to avoid the minefield at the entrance to Long Island Sound. Following three days of load-lightening, she was finally assisted by tugs back to the Navy Yard for further repairs. Repairs completed in December, she departed New York on 30 January, arriving at Scapa Flow, the British anchorage in the Orkney Islands off Scotland on 11 February to join with the 6th Battle Squadron of Britain's Grand Fleet.

The main role of *Texas* with the Grand Fleet was in support of convoys and the reinforcement of blockades in the North Sea when German big-gun warships threatened. Her duties began five days after she arrived in Scapa Flow. *Texas* and the other vessels of the Grand Fleet came within sight of the German fleet on 25 April, but the German ships returned to their base rather than engaging with the British.

In the first few days of July, *Texas* escorted American minelayers in the expansion of the mined area, followed by wargames and tactical exercises. She continued in such operations for the remainder of the war and sailed with the Grand Fleet to meet the surrendering German fleet.

In December 1938, *Texas* was among the first U.S. Navy warships to be fitted with the new RCA-manufactured shipborne radar installations. From September 1939, she operated as part of the Neutrality Patrol, America's attempt to keep the Second World War out of the western hemisphere. As the U.S. edged towards participation in the war, *Texas* escorted convoys bringing Lend-Lease matériel to the United Kingdom and on 1 February U.S. Navy Admiral Ernest King brought his flag aboard her as Commander-in-Chief of the Atlantic Fleet.

With American entry in the war after the 7 December 1941 attack by the Japanese on Pearl Harbor, *Texas* participated in many convoy escort missions in the Atlantic, through early 1944 when she began training for the Normandy invasion. She was designated Bombardment Force Flagship for Omaha Beach in the Western Task Force on 6 June, D-Day. Together with the battleship *Arkansas*, the French light cruisers *Georges Leygues* and *Montcalm*, the British light cruiser HMS *Glasgow*, the British destroyers HMS *Tanatside*, *Talybont*, and *Melbreak*, and the American destroyers *Baldwin*, *Carmick*, *Doyle*, *Emmons*, *Frankford*, *Harding*, *McCook*, *Satterlee*, and *Thompson*, *Texas* took part in the bombardment of the Omaha Beach area.

At three in the morning of 6 June, *Texas* and the cruiser *Glasgow* were in their initial firing position some 12,000 yards off Pointe du Hoc, a part of an Allied flotilla of 702 warships that included seven battleships and five heavy cruisers.

The battleship big guns commenced shelling the Normandy beaches at 5:50 a.m. By the end of the barrage, at 6:24 a.m., the guns of *Texas* had fired 255 fourteen-inch shells at the Pointe du Hoc target at the rate of 7.5 shells per minute. She then shifted her main guns to fire on the western edge of Omaha Beach near the town of Vierville. Later, the fire of her main guns was directed inland onto German reinforcement activities, gun batteries, and strong points.

At midday, the overall position of the Allied assault on Omaha was seriously weakened by their inability to advance badly needed armour and artillery units onto the beach. *Texas* and some of the destroyers then moved much closer in to the shore, some of them nearly running aground in the effort, to bring increased gunfire down on the enemy there. *Texas* came to within 3,000 yards of the shoreline, laying heavy fire on German positions and fortifications, as well as an anti-aircraft battery west of Vierville.

Struck from the naval register on 30 April 1948, *Texas* is the first, and oldest of the eight surviving American battleships to have become floating museums—the others being *Alabama, Iowa, Massachusetts, Missouri, New Jersey, North Carolina,* and *Wisconsin*.

She would revolutionize the battleship concept and naval sea power. HMS *Dreadnought* came into service in 1906, instantly and dramatically advancing naval and battleship technology and establishing an iconic presence among all warships. The battleships that had come before *Dreadnought* were thereafter known as pre-dreadnoughts, and were plainly obsolete.

It was Royal Navy Admiral Sir Jacky Fisher who was known as "the father of the dreadnought". He it was who ordered the original design studies for an all big-gun battleship, armed with twelve-inch guns and capable of twenty-four miles an hour.

Dreadnought displaced 18,410 tons, was 527 feet long with a beam of eighty-two feet and a draft of more than twenty-nine feet. She had a range of 7,620 miles at a speed of twelve mph, and was manned by a crew of up to 810. Her armament was five twelve-inch guns, twenty-seven twelve-pounder guns, and five eighteen-inch torpedo tubes. Admiral Fisher formed a Committee on Designs in 1904 to evaluate design proposals for his dream battleship and participate in the refinement of that design. As its president, Fisher ruled over the committee, keeping it firmly on course towards the development of the vessel he so wanted. During the development of *Dreadnought*, the two battleships of the *Lord Nelson* class were under construction. *Dreadnought* would be considerably larger than the *Lord Nelson* ships. She was to be built with a complete double hull bottom, and would be the first battleship to be propelled by steam turbines rather than traditional reciprocating triple-expansion steam engines.

HMS *Dreadnought* served as the flagship of the Royal Navy Home Fleet from 1907 through 1911.

below: The USS *Texas*; top right: HMS *Dreadnought*.

By the time the First World War began, *Dreadnought* had become the flagship of the 4th Battle Squadron, then based at Scapa Flow. Despite her fame and prominence as the pioneering vessel of her type, and the fact that she had been designed to engage, overwhelm and thoroughly defeat enemy battleships, she never actually experienced such adventures in her career at sea. Her one claim to combat fame resulted from an encounter with the German submarine *SM U-29* which was under the command of Kapitän-Leutnant Otto Weddigen, on 18 March 1915 when the U-boat broke the surface immediately in front of *Dreadnought*, having just fired a torpedo at the dreadnought battleship HMS *Neptune* in Pentland Firth. After a brief chase, *Dreadnought* caught up with and rammed *U-29*, becoming the only battleship ever to sink a submarine.

The development and construction of *Dreadnought* quickly influenced all major naval fleets, setting off an arms race among them and spurring construction of many dreadnought-like battleships the world over. In April 1963, the seventh ship to bear the name HMS *Dreadnought*, a nuclear-powered submarine of the Royal Navy, entered service.

The French pre-dreadnought battleship *Suffren*, named after Vice Admiral Pierre André de Suffren de Saint Tropez, was 413 feet long with a beam of seventy feet and a draught of twenty-seven feet. With a displacement of 12,432 tons, a top speed of twenty mph, and a range of 4,700 miles at fourteen mph, *Suffren* carried a normal complement of 668 men. Her armament comprised four twelve-inch

left: The USS *Nevada* firing her main guns in a practice exercise; bottom: The *Nevada* in drydock at Pearl Harbor Navy Yard circa 1935; below: French Admiral Pierre Andre de Suffren.

guns, ten 6.5-inch guns, eight 3.9-inch guns, twenty 1.9-inch Hotchkiss guns, two 1.5-inch guns, and four eighteen-inch torpedo tubes.

Suffren played a part in the action at the Dardenelles in the First World War in 1914 and later, in 1915 when she became the flagship of Rear Admiral Émile Guépratte. There, with the assistance of the pre-dreadnought battleship Bouvet, she bombarded the Turkish fort of Kum Kale and later managed, with the help of Gaulois, to come to the aid of the British pre-dreadnought HMS Vengeance which was taking fire from the Turks. Vengeance was then able to safely withdraw from her predicament.

On 18 March, in another major attack on the Turkish forts by the British warships, the French pre-dreadnoughts steamed through the British ranks and engaged the enemy forts at closer range. In doing so, Suffren was hit by an enemy shell that tore the roof from the port casemate, killing the entire gun crew. Then another shell bored through the bow causing a flood in the forward turret. The nearby Bouvet then struck a mine, exploded and sank in less than a minute. Suffren's crew was able to rescue seventy-five of Bouvet's crew members before escorting the severely damaged Gaulois away from the Dardenelles.

In the morning of 26 November, Suffren was steaming some fifty-seven miles off the Portuguese coast near Lisbon when she was hit by a torpedo from the submarine SM U-52. The strike set off a magazine explosion and Suffren sank in seconds with the loss of her entire crew.

SMS König was the lead ship of the four König class dreadnought battleships built for the German Imperial Navy. Launched in 1913, König was named in honour of King William II of Württemberg. The König was 575 feet long with a beam of ninety-six feet nine inches, and a draught of thirty feet. She carried a ship's complement of 1,136 men, had a range of 8,000 miles at twelve knots, and top speed of twenty-four mph. She was armed with ten twelve-inch guns, fourteen 5.9-inch guns, ten 3.5-inch guns, and five 19.7-inch torpedo tubes.

Completing her sea trials in November 1914, König was attached to III Battle Squadron of the German High Seas Fleet, in which she sailed in support of Rear Admiral Franz von Hipper's battlecruisers. In late January 1915, she and the other ships of III Squadron conducted maneuvers, gunnery and torpedo training in the Baltic before heading into the North Sea.

On 24 April 1916, König and her sister ships accompanied the German battlecruiser force from the Jade Estuary on a mission to bombard the east coast of England, specifically Lowestoft. When approaching Yarmouth, they ran into British cruisers of the Harwich Force, which withdrew after a brief artillery exchange. The German ships then retreated after reports of British submarines being in the area.

König was one of the key German warships participating in the Battle of Jutland, the main sea battle of the war. Her role is covered in the chapter Jutland. With the end of the war in 1918, the majority of the German High Seas Fleet was interned in the British base at Scapa Flow, where they remained, their big guns disabled, during the period of the Versailles Treaty negotiations. After the German surrender, their fleet was placed under the command of the German Rear Admiral Ludwig von Reuter. On the morning of 21 June, Reuter ordered the ships of the captured fleet scuttled, including König, which sank at 2:00 p.m.

The USS Nevada (BB-36) represented a significant step forward in the development of dreadnought technology, including gun turrets with three big guns, the 'all or nothing' armour principle, and oil fuel

left: The U.S. Navy battleship *New York*, and the *Florida*, *Delaware*, and *Wyoming* were sent to join the British Grand Fleet with America's entry into the First World War in 1917.

instead of coal. Nearly all future American battleships would be designed and built with those features.

Named for the state of Nevada, the ship was laid down on 4 November 1912, launched on 11 July 1914 and commissioned on 11 March 1916. Displacing 27,500 tons, she was 583 feet long with a beam of ninety-five feet and a draught of twenty-eight feet six inches. Her top speed was twenty-four mph and her range was 5,890 miles at fourteen mph. Her ultimate ship's complement numbered 2,220, and her armament consisted of ten fourteen-inch guns, twenty-one five-inch guns, and four twenty-one-inch torpedo tubes. She was the first U.S. Navy battleship to have triple gun turrets, a single funnel, and oil-fired steam powerplants.

With the U.S. entry into the First World War in 1917, four coal-burning American battleships, *Florida*, *Delaware*, *New York*, and *Wyoming*, were sent across the Atlantic to join the British Grand Fleet. They were later joined by the *Texas*, but *Nevada* was prevented from being sent due to a shortage of fuel oil in Britain. She finally sailed for the UK in August 1918. For the rest of the war, she operated with *Oklahoma* and *Utah*, escorting convoys to Britain against the threat of German warships.

After the war *Nevada* served in the U.S. Pacific Fleet, and was at anchorage in Pearl Harbor in the morning of 7 December when the Japanese surprise attack occurred. As her engineers raised steam power during the attack, she was struck by a torpedo, causing some flooding and a slight list which was corrected through counter-flooding. At 8:40 a.m. she got under way, but as she maneuvered in the narrow harbour channel, she became a prime target for the second wave of enemy aircraft, which hoped to sink her and block the channel for perhaps many months. In the ongoing action, gunners aboard *Nevada* shot down four Japanese planes. At 9:50 she was hit by five bombs, causing many explosions and serious fires. Fortunately, the main magazines were empty at the time of the attack, as ammunition loading was set to take place later in the day.

As the situation aboard *Nevada* deteriorated, she received orders to head for the west side of the Ford Island base in the middle of the harbour, to prevent her being sunk in the channel. Her crew then grounded her off Hospital Point and her gunners brought down three additional enemy aircraft.

In the raid, her crew suffered sixty men killed and 109 wounded. Her own end came on 31 July 1948 when she was used as the object of target practice by the gun crews of the battleship USS *Iowa* and two other warships. She was not sunk in the exercise and was then sent to the bottom of the sea by an aerial torpedo.

Surprise!

Scores of Japanese fighter-bombers, torpedo-bombers, and fighters appeared in loose formations low over the lush green hills of northern Oahu in the Hawaiian Islands on that bright December Sunday morning in 1941. Surprise clearly understated the common emotion of the residents and the American naval and military personnel there. Confusion and chaos ruled. Death and destruction on a large scale had arrived.

Millions of Americans had been opposed to the new League of Nations and the Treaty of Versailles created after the end of the First World War. Their fundamental isolationist perspective had led to the passage by the U.S. Congress of the Neutrality Acts of 1935 and 1937 which radically restricted aid to any belligerent countries. Such was the intensity of American opposition to involvement in a new European war, openly and actively opposed by the America First Committee that, when U.S. President Franklin Roosevelt was running for a third term of office in October 1940, he pledged "I shall say it again and again. Your boys are not going to be sent into any foreign wars." As editorialized in Harper's Magazine, "America may be sick with pity for the victims of totalitarian aggression in Europe, but we are thankful we are out of it and hardly afraid of being dragged in."

Such was not the case, however, with reference to activities in the Pacific. The relationship between Japan and the United States had deteriorated dramatically in the 1930s. Japan perceived itself, significantly, as the only Asian nation to have, through their own efforts and capabilities advanced to a level of modern industrialization sufficient to justifiably and rightfully emerge as leader of the Asian countries. She still smarted with frustration and humiliation resulting from the Anglo-American disarmament agreements after the First World War, and the economic penalties she was subjected to following her 1937 attack on China.

As she entered the decade of the 1940s, Japan had an enormous requirement for raw materials and agricultural resources, in particular those of Burma, Malaya, the Dutch East Indies, and China, and that interest in China, would lead to ultimate conflict with the United States, which had allied itself with the new Chinese Republic. Japan's persistent aggressive behaviour towards China brought an angry reaction from the United States, expressed through the denial of oil and strategic metals supplies to the Japanese and this in turn led Japanese leaders on a course to war with the U.S. That course was pursued through its naval air attack on Pearl Harbor, Hawaii, on 7 December 1941, and through attacks on the Philippines, Burma, Malaya, and the Dutch East Indies, as well as the Japanese occupation of French Indo-China. These Japanese agressions involved combat with the Dutch and British navies.

In the surprise attack on American warships, naval and air facilities at Pearl Harbor, some 400 aircraft had been launched from the flight decks of six aircraft carriers of the Imperial Japanese Navy. The carriers *Akagi*, *Hiryu*, *Kaga*, *Shokaku*, *Soryu* and *Ziukaku*, under the overall command of Vice Admiral Chuichi Nagumo, had brought their aircraft and air wing personnel to within relatively easy striking distance of the American naval base on Oahu where much of the U.S. Navy battleship fleet was at anchor. In the attack, eight of the big warships were severely damaged. Of them, *Arizona* and *Oklahoma* were damaged beyond repair. *West Virginia*, *California*, and *Nevada* were sufficiently wrecked to put them out of action for many months, and *Pennsylvania*, *Maryland*, and *Tennessee* also suffered significant damage. Twenty-nine Japanese aircraft were lost in the raid. Additional American naval losses

The U.S. Navy battleships *West Virginia*, *Tennessee*, and *Arizona* burn furiously during the surprise attack by aircraft of the Imperial Japanese Navy on American ships and shore facilities in Pearl Harbor, Hawaii, on Sunday, 7 December 1941, the attack which drew America into the war.

included three destroyers sunk and three light cruisers damaged. 164 of the 394 U.S. aircraft on Oahu were destroyed, with a further 159 damaged. Human casualties amounted to 2,395 military personnel and civilians killed, with 1,178 wounded.

As the exultant Japanese air crews returned from the raid to their carriers, many of them urged an immediate second strike in which to complete the devastation they had started at Pearl. But the absence of the three principal American Pacific-region aircraft carriers, *Enterprise*, *Lexington*, and *Saratoga*, caused Admiral Nagumo to take a different tack. On 7 December, the day of the Japanese attack on Pearl, *Enterprise* sailed in the lead of Task Force 8, returning to Oahu from Wake Island. TF-8 was a bit more than 200 miles west of Pearl. *Lexington* and her escort vessels were about 500 miles southeast of Midway Island, and *Saratoga* was about to arrive at NAS North Island, San Diego in the afternoon of the 7th.

In the two hours of Admiral Nagumo's aerial attack on the American naval facilities and battleships at Pearl Harbor, the amount of death and destruction delivered by the air wings of his carriers served to galvanize Americans and the American President and Congress. In the early afternoon of 7 December the President was informed by his Secretary of War, Henry Stimson, of the Japanese attack. After meetings in the afternoon with his military advisors, he dictated to his secretary, Grace Tully, the text of the message he would deliver to the Congress the next day. President Roosevelt spoke to the Congress and the nation at 12:30 p.m. on 8 December, and asked the Congress for a declaration of war on the Empire of Japan. The Senate and the House of Representatives responded with a unanimous vote in support of the war. The only dissenting vote was that of Jeannette Rankin, the first female member of Congress and a lifelong pacifist.

The President's speech: "Yesterday, December 7th 1941—a date which will live in infamy—the United States of America was suddenly and deliberately attacked by naval and air forces of the Empire of Japan.

"The United States was at peace with that Nation and, at the solicitation of Japan, was still in conversation with its Government and its Emperor looking toward the maintenance of peace in the Pacific. Indeed, one hour after Japanese air squadrons had commenced bombing in the American Island of Oahu, the Japanese Ambassador to the United States and his colleague delivered to our Secretary of State a formal reply to a recent American message. And while this reply stated that it seemed useless to continue the existing diplomatic negotiations, it contained no threat or hint of war or of armed attack.

"It will be recorded that the distance of Hawaii from Japan makes it obvious that the attack was deliberately planned many days or even weeks ago. During the intervening time the Japanese Government has deliberately sought to deceive the United States by false statements and expressions of hope for continued peace.

"The attack yesterday on the Hawaiian Islands has caused severe damage to American naval and military forces. I regret to tell you that very many American lives have been lost. In addtion American ships have been reported torpedoed on the high seas between San Francisco and Honolulu.

"Yesterday the Japanese Government also launched an attack against Malaya. Last night Japanese forces attacked Hong Kong. Last night Japanese forces attacked Guam. Last night Japanese forces attacked the Philippine Islands. Last night the Japanese attacked Wake Island. And this morning the Japanese attacked Midway Island.

"Japan has, therefore, undertaken a surprise offensive extending throughout the Pacific area. The

The burning hulk of the American battleship *California* minutes after the early morning raid on Pearl Harbor.

facts of yesterday and today speak for themselves. The people of the United States have already formed their opinions and well understand the implications to the very life and safety of our Nation.

"As Commander in Chief of the Army and Navy I have directed that all measures be taken for our defense.

"But always will our whole Nation remember the character of the onslaught against us.

"No matter how long it may take us to overcome this premeditated invasion, the American people in their righteous might will win through to absolute victory. I believe that I interpret the will of the Congress and of the people when I assert that we will not only defend ourselves to the uttermost but will make it very certain that this form of treachery shall never again endanger us.

"Hostilities exist. There is no blinking at the fact that our people, our territory, and our interests are in grave danger.

"With confidence in our armed forces—with the unbounding determination of our people—we will gain the inevitable triumph—so help us God.

"I ask that the Congress declare that since the unprovoked and dastardly attack by Japan on Sunday, December 7th, 1941, a state of war has existed between the United States and the Japanese Empire."

For her part, Japan had prepared her declaration of war on the United States and the British Empire, dated 7 December 1941 and released it on the front pages of all Japanese newspapers in the evening editions of 8 December. Originally it was not the intention of the Japanese High Command that their attack on Pearl Harbor begin before Japan's representatives in Washington had notified the United States government that she was pulling out of any further peace negotiations. The High Command had planned to adhere to the conventions of war, but their 5,000-word message to their men in the U.S. capitol took much longer to translate than anyone had anticipated, making it impossible for the Japanese Ambassador to the United States to personally deliver it to U.S. Secretary of State Cordell Hull in time. Though the attack on Pearl was planned to begin at least thirty minutes after the notification in Washington, in fact it preceded the ambassador's appointment with Hull. Actually, the lengthy translation was worded in such a way that it neither severed the negotiations with America or declared war. Britain, America's great ally in the war, had declared war on Japan more than nine hours before the U.S. declaration of war. Prime Minister Winston Churchill had acted, having promised to declare war within the hour of a Japanese attack on the United States, and because of Japanese attacks then under way against Singapore, Hong Kong, and Malaya.

The Japanese declaration of war: "By the grace of Heaven, Emperor of Japan [Emperor Showa], seated on the throne occupied by the same dynasty from time immemorial, enjoin upon ye, Our loyal and brave subjects: We hereby declare War on the United States of America and the British Empire. The men and officers of Our Army and Navy shall do their utmost in prosecuting the war. Our public servants of various departments shall perform faithfully and diligently their respective duties; the entire nation with a united will shall mobilize their total strength so that nothing will miscarry in the attainment of Our war aims.

"To ensure the stability of East Asia and to contribute to world peace is the far-sighted policy which was formulated by Our Great Illustrious Imperial Grandsire [Emperor Meiji] and Our Great Imperial Sire succeeding Him [Emperor Taisho], and which We lay constantly to heart. To cultivate friendship among nations and to enjoy prosperity in common with all nations, has always been the guiding prin-

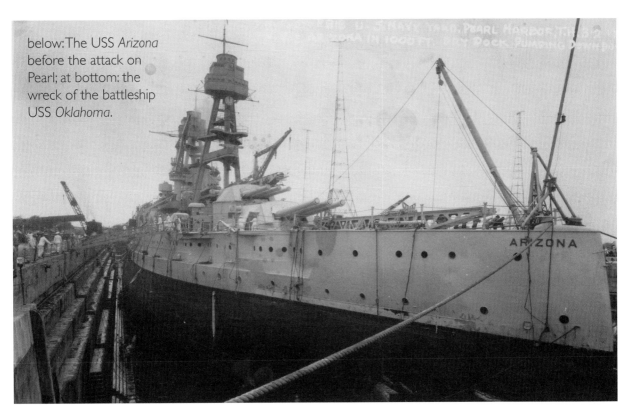

below: The USS *Arizona* before the attack on Pearl; at bottom: the wreck of the battleship USS *Oklahoma*.

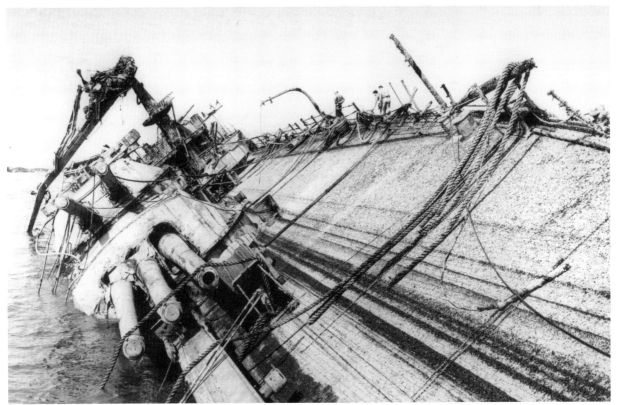

clockwise from upper left: The USS *Iowa* shelling the Korean coast in 1960; The main guns of the *Missouri* in Pearl Harbor; A reunion at war's end; U.S. President Harry S. Truman after Japanese surrender in August 1945.

ciple of Our Empire's foreign policy. It has been truly unavoidable and far from Our wishes that Our Empire has been brought to cross swords with America and Britain. More than four years have passed since China, failing to comprehend the true intentions of Our Empire, and recklessly courting trouble, disturbed the peace of East Asia and compelled Our Empire to take up arms. Although there has been reestablished the National Government of China, with which Japan had effected neighborly intercourse and cooperation, the regime which has survived in Chungking, relying upon American and British protection, still continues its fratricidal opposition. Eager for the realization of their inordinate ambition to dominate the Orient, both America and Britain, giving support to the Chunking regime, have aggrivated the disturbances in East Asia. Moreover these two Powers, inducing other countries to follow suit, increased military preparations on all sides of Our Empire to challenge Us. They have obstructed by every means Our peaceful commerce and finally resorted to a direct severance of economic relations, menacing gravely the existence of Our Empire. Patiently have We waited and long have We endured, in the hope that our government might retrieve the situation in peace. But Our adversaries, showing not the least spirit of conciliation, have unduly delayed a settlement; and in the meantime they have intensified the economic and political pressure to compel thereby Our Empire to submission. This trend of affairs, would, if left unchecked, not only nullify Our Empire's efforts of many years for the sake of the stabilization of East Asia, but also endanger the very existence of Our nation. The situation being such as it is, Our Empire, for its existence and self-defense has no other recourse but to appeal to arms and to crush every obstacle in its path.

"The hallowed spirits of Our Imperial Ancestors guarding Us from above, We rely upon the loyalty and courage of Our subjects in Our confident expectation that the task bequeathed by Our forefathers will be carried forward and that the sources of evil will be speedily eradicated and an enduring peace immutably established in East Asia, preserving thereby the glory of Our Empire.

"In witness whereof, we have hereunto set our hand and caused the Grand Seal of the Empire to be affixed at the Imperial Palace, Tokyo, this seventh day of the 12th month of the 15th year of Showa, corresponding to the 2,602nd year from the accession to the throne of Emperor Jimmu."

The fact that the three Pacific-based American carriers were not in Pearl Harbor at the time of the attack was greatly disappointing to Japanese naval planners and Nagumo. But the admiral believed his force had achieved sufficient success in the raid, destroying or crippling the bulk of the American battleship fleet in the Pacific, and elected to take his carriers away from the staging area and into other action—against the British in Burma, Hong Kong, and Malaya, against the Americans in the Philippines, and against the Dutch in the Netherlands East Indies. In Japan, the leadership were generally pleased with the results of the Pearl Harbor attack, viewing it as a reasonably good start to their Pacific war, and felt quite comfortable with the attack based on what they perceived as many years of abuse and humiliation by the United States and the colonial empires of Europe. The disarmament arrangements, largely controlled by the Americans and British following the First World War, had been forced upon the Japanese and they still smarted from what they saw as considerable economic penalties meted out on them for their 1937 attack on China.

The Americans, anxious to strike an early and highly visible blow on the Japanese enemy, made plans for an audacious attack of their own to be launched in April 1942. In one of the war's first and most effective examples of powerful psychological warfare coupled with conventional aerial attack, sixteen Army Air Force North American B-25 Mitchell bombers were transported on the aircraft carrier

Hornet to a launch point within 800 miles of the Japanese home islands. From there the fully-loaded bombers, under the command of then-Lt. Col. Jimmy Doolittle, flew to hit four cities including Tokyo. The land-based Mitchells could not return to the carrier and the plan called for them to continue on to airfields in China, but all were compelled to crash-land or ditch when they ran out of fuel before reaching the Chinese fields.

As bombing raids of the Second World War went, the Doolittle Raid inflicted little real damage on the Japanese populace or infrastructure, but in terms of psychological value its impact was enormous. The Japanese High Command, to say nothing of the Japanese people as a whole, were genuinely shocked and unsettled by the seemingly incredible experience of witnessing bombing raids on their cities; something they had never seriously contemplated. That shock produced a sea change in their philosophy and conduct of the war, from one of blatant territorial conquest throughout Southeast Asia, to expanding their effort to control much of the Pacific region. So gravely did they perceive this new threat to the security and safety of the Japanese emperor, and the depth of this insult to the honour of Japan, that their entire approach to the conflict was influenced and modified.

Just as the Germans had determined that England would have to be invaded and occupied in the autumn of 1940, to prevent its future use as key base from which the British, and later the Americans, could conduct a punishing campaign of strategic bombing against Germany, so the Japanese thought it essential to capture and occupy the island of New Guinea, near Australia, to deny the Americans the use of Australia as a strategic base against them. They had hoped to create a decisive naval victory at Pearl Harbor, but in the effort had failed to destroy the U.S. Navy battleship force, or the vital oil tank farm at Pearl and the submarine base there, or, most significantly, the American carrier force which would be back to make them pay dearly for that failure.

The determination of the Japanese to take New Guinea led to a major confrontation in early May off the island, the Battle of the Coral Sea. Had they achieved victory in the battle, Australia would have been open to Japanese attack and occupation. The battle was almost entirely fought by carrier aircraft of both sides and, in fact, was not a clear victory for either, but in denying the Japanese a clear-cut triumph there, the American navy forced the Imperial Japanese Navy into a probable drawn-out war at sea that they might well lose. Now the vital goal of the IJN was to locate, engage and destroy the carriers of the U.S. Navy. Failing that, they and the Japanese High Command, could look forward to greater, more devastating attacks on the home islands.

The next important phase of the Pacific war came on 4 June, the most significant battle of the Pacific campaign. It was the first real revenge the Americans had been able to take for the Japanese attack on Pearl Harbor. The Battle of Midway proved to be the turning point in the Pacific war and the largest and most significant demonstration to date of the transition from the battleship as principal capital ship of the great navies, to the aircraft carrier as the inheritor of that role. At Midway, which was the last major United States military facility in the western Pacific to escape capture by the Japanese, the Americans had set a trap to force the big carriers of the Imperial Japanese Fleet to fight. With a less effective Intelligence capability than that of the Americans, the Japanese Navy was convinced that Midway Island was essentially undefended and no real threat to its carrier fleet. Admiral Nagumo confidently took the six aircraft carriers with which he had launched the Pearl Harbor attack, to a point from which they could mount a major strike on Midway. Admiral Raymond Spruance, who would earn a place in the Battle of Midway as one of the greatest admirals in American naval

Nagumo's carriers with just three of his own, the *Enterprise, Hornet,* and *Yorktown.* But he had one great advantage. The government code-breakers in Washington had deciphered the Japanese naval code and provided Spruance with the exact location of Nagumo's fleet, whereas the Japanese admiral was unaware of the American carriers being in the region of Midway.

When hostilities began near the island, it appeared that the Japanese had the upper hand, as they managed to shoot down all of the attacking American torpedo bombers in the early encounter. By the end of the day, however, the American carrier-based aircraft had destroyed four of the six Japanese carriers in dive-bombing attacks, virtually ending any future threat from the Japanese naval air force. While the Japanese struggled to continue their Pacific campaign without replacements for the carriers they had lost at Midway, the U.S. Navy was busy launching a massive fleet of new, formidable *Essex*-class carriers with which to bring the war to the home islands of Japan by 1945.

One of the best and brightest members of the Japanese military leaders, Admiral Isoroku Yamamoto, had served his government as a Japanese naval attaché in Washington before the war. He had warned the Japanese Army Staff officers of what Japan would face should her forces fail to completely subdue U.S. forces at the start of the war . . . that the immense capacity of American war industry would utterly overwhelm Japanese forces and defeat her.

The capsized USS *Oklahoma* and the USS *Maryland* after the Pearl Harbor attack of 7 December 1941.

Graf Spee

The Panzerschiff (pocket battleship) *Admiral Graf Spee* was a part of the German Navy in the Second World War. Named after Admiral Maximilian von Spee, the former commander of the German East Asia Squadron, which fought the Battles of the Falkland Islands and Coronel in the First World War, the *Graf Spee* was laid down in October 1932, launched 30 June 1934, and commissioned 6 January 1936. The Treaty of Versailles at the end of the First World War had stipulated various limitations on the size, speed, equipment, performance and capability of future warships of the German Navy. The limitations in place for one of *Graf Spee*'s type included a displacement of 10,000 tons, which she greatly exceeded at 16,280 tons. *Graf Spee* was powerfully armed with six eleven-inch big guns, eight 5.9-inch guns, and eight twenty-one-inch torpedo tubes. With such armament, and a top speed of thirty-two mph, she was more than a match for her opponents in the French and British navies. 610 feet long, with a beam of seventy-one feet and a draught of twenty-four feet, she had a range of 10,200 miles at twenty-three mph. Her ship's complement included thirty-three officers and 586 men, later evolved to thirty officers and 1,040 men.

Hans Wilhelm Langsdorff had joined the German Imperial Navy in 1912 at the age of eighteen and saw action in the Battle of Jutland four years later. His initial command was that of a minesweeper, shortly after Jutland, followed by a four-year stint with the Ministry of Defence in Berlin. He was made a Kapitän zur See in 1938 and made commander of the *Graf Spee* which, together with her sister ships, *Admiral Scheer* and *Deutschland*, were considered the finest warships in the German Navy at the time. These three ships, high-speed, diesel-powered giants, were admired and respected by all the other great naval powers, but they were also more vulnerable than they may have seemed at first glance, due to their relatively light belt and deck armour.

On 21 August 1939, a few days before the war with Britain began, *Graf Spee* was sent steaming from the harbour of Wilhelmshaven on a voyage to the South Atlantic, her "raider cruise", assigned to hunt down, attack and sink the merchant ships running along the vital shipping lanes to Britain. In that capacity, she ran down and sank nine British freighters for a total tonnage of 50,000.

While in command of *Graf Spee*, Captain Langsdorff, a man of integrity and one who respected rules, unlike some of his colleagues, made a point of adhering strictly to the rules of the International Hague Conventions. He made sure that the *Graf Spee* prominently displayed her battle ensign every time she came upon an enemy vessel to be attacked. He immediately signalled this warning to the merchant vessel crew: "Stop. Do not use wireless or we will fire." He always saw to the evacuation of the target vessel's crewmen before giving the order to sink the ship, and none of the sixty-two prisoners that he took from the ships he sank were harmed under his care.

The *Graf Spee* spent her first three months at sea in the conduct of extensive sea trials to prepare her for war service. Her first commander was Kapitän zur See Conrad Patzig, who in 1937 was replaced by Kapitän zur See Walter Warzecha. On completion of a lengthy training period, she joined the fleet and and soon was made the Flagship of the German Navy. With the opening of the Spanish Civil War in 1936, *Graf Spee* was deployed as a part of non-intervention patrols on the Republican-controlled coast of Spain between August 1936 and May 1937. During her return voyage to Germany she made a port call in England to represent Germany in the Coronation Review at Spithead for King George VI.

The German pocket battleship *Graf Spee* in harbour circa 1936.

Thereafter, she participated in two further non-intervention patrols off Spain through February 1938, after which Kapitän zur See Hans Langsdorff assumed her command. He then took her on series of goodwill visits to ports that included Tangier and Vigo, followed by a stretch of extensive fleet maneuvers near Germany, until her August 1939 departure for the South Atlantic.

After the Second World War broke out in September, the German Chanchellor Adolf Hitler ordered his navy to begin commerce raiding of Allied merchant shipping. He somewhat hedged his bet, however, on the chance that the British might yet agree to some sort of peace settlement after his conquest of Poland. He saw that Langsdorff was specifically instructed to keep to prize rules, requiring *Graf Spee* to stop and search all ships for contraband before sinking them and to see their crews safely evacuated before taking action against the merchant ships. He was ordered to avoid combat and to change the ship's position frequently.

While under way, *Graf Spee* rendezvoused with the German supply ship *Altmark*, for replenishing on 1 September. On the 11th, the pilot of *Graf Spee*'s Arado reconnaissance floatplane sighted the British heavy cruiser HMS *Cumberland*, which was nearing the two German ships. Langsdorff then ordered both German vessels to leave the area at high speed and they successfully evaded the British warship. A few weeks later, on 26 September, Hitler finally gave the order permitting German naval vessels to attack Allied merchant ships without restriction. Four days later, *Graf Spee* was involved in the sinking of another Allied merchant ship, the steamer *Clement*, after which Langsdorff had a distress signal sent to the naval station at Pernambuco to arrange for the rescue of the *Clement*"s crew in their lifeboats. Following this incident, the British Admiralty issued an emergency warning to all merchant shipping in the South Atlantic that a German surface raider was in the region.

This led to the formation of eight groups of British and French warships assigned to hunt down

German pocket battleship *Admiral Graf Spee* in Kiel canal.

and sink *Graf Spee*. Among the vessels taking part in the hunt were the Royal Navy aircraft carriers *Ark Royal*, *Eagle*, and *Hermes*, the French carrier *Béarn*, the British cruiser *Renown*, the French battleships *Dunkerque* and *Strasbourg*, together with sixteen additional cruisers. The British Force G squadron assigned was commanded by Commodore Henry Harwood and made up of the cruisers *Cumberland* and *Exeter*, and was supported by the light cruisers *Achilles* and *Ajax*. Harwood detached *Cumberland* to patrol the Falkland Islands area as his other three cruisers patrolled off the River Plate area. As the British and French hunter groups were forming, the crew of *Graf Spee* were dealing with two more Allied merchant ships, the *Ashlea* and the *Newton Beech*. Langsdorff was then using the *Newton Beech* to house prisoners he had captured, but the *Newton Beech* was proving too slow to keep up with *Graf Spee* and Langsdorff had to order it sunk after transferring the prisoners to *Graf Spee*. Then, on 10 October, *Graf Spee* captured the merchant steamer *Huntsman*, but with no more room to accommodate prisoners aboard the pocket battleship, Langsdorff had to make other arrangements. On 15 October, *Graf Spee* rendezvoused with *Altmark* to refuel and the next day, the prisoners on board *Graf Spee*, and those on *Huntsman*, were all transferred to *Altmark*. Langsdorff later sank *Huntsman*.

The merchant steamer *Trevanion* crossed paths with *Graf Spee* on 22 October and was sunk by her. By early November the pocket battleship had steamed about 30,000 miles and was in need of major engine servicing. On 15 November she met up with and sank the tanker *Africa Shell*. She went to meet *Altmark* for a lengthy replenishment and rest period of about a week during which the crew constructed a dummy gun turret on her forecastle as well as a second funnel to substantially change her silhouette and hopefully confuse Allied shipping about her identity.

The next significant event in the career of *Graf Spee* occurred when her floatplane pilot sighted the merchant vessel *Doric Star* and Captain Langsdorff had a warning shot fired across her bow telling her to stop. Before doing so, the *Doric Star* captain managed to send out a distress signal which caused Commodore Harwood to take his three cruisers to the mouth of the River Plate, in the belief that *Graf Spee*'s next target would be there. In the evening of 5 December the *Graf Spee* found and sank the steamer *Tairoa* and on the following day, Langsdorff again met up with *Altmark* to transfer an additional 140 prisoners from both *Doric Star* and *Tairoa*. *Graf Spee*'s last victim of the period was the freighter *Streonshalh* on the night of 7 December. Along with her prize prisoners, the freighter yielded secret documents which informed Captain Langsdorff about Allied shipping routes and, with that information, he elected to take *Graf Spee* to the area immediately off Montevideo, Uruguay. On the way there, the ship's reconnaissance floatplane became unrepairable and was discarded as were the artificial gun turret and funnel the crew had built, on the possibility that they might hinder the ship in a coming battle.

13 December 1939. A lookout in *Graf Spee* spotted a vessel on the horizon causing Captain Langsdorff to pursue it for identification at 5:30 a.m. At this point *Graf Spee* was about 200 miles off the estuary of the River Plate, a feature that separates Uruguay from Argentina. The pocket battleship rapidly closed on the unidentified ship and was able to confirm her identity as the French liner *Formose*. As the two ships closed on one another, a third was sighted from *Graf Spee*, the Royal Navy cruiser HMS *Exeter*, whose crew had picked up a distress signal from *Formose*, and was rushing to her assistance. Now the British cruiser was sending a signal to the other cruisers in the area, HMNZS *Achilles* and HMS *Ajax*, to join her in the pursuit of *Graf Spee*. As the three cruisers joined up and went after *Graf Spee*, which had turned south, the *Formose* left the scene.

Graf Spee was low on fuel and Langsdorff, wanting to avoid combat with the enemy warships in his low fuel state, had altered course to try and evade them. But the enemy vessels manouevered to cut off his escape and his only option was to stand and fight. So he ordered his crew to battle stations and sent his ship towards the enemy at full speed. He intended to destroy *Exeter* before the other two enemy cruisers could engage him. He ordered the gun crews to open fire with *Graf Spee*'s eleven-inch guns as soon as he was within range and before *Exeter*'s eight-inch guns could be brought to bear on *Graf Spee*.

A shell from *Graf Spee* found its mark, destroying the bridge of *Exeter* and killing everyone there except the captain, one other officer, and a midshipman. The wrecked *Exeter* was seriously crippled, but now within range of the German pocket battleship. The gun crews of the British cruiser opened fire just as *Exeter* received yet another punishing round damaging her badly enough to force her retirement from the action.

The author/historian Joseph Gilbey wrote in the book *Langsdorff of the Graf Spee, Prince of Honour*: "There is little to compare to the hellish brutality of a sea battle. Men are entrapped in a tight steel box, a warship. They are beyond sight of land, floating in untold fathoms of sea-water. Separated by miles of rolling ocean, combatting warships throw tons of high explosives at each other. It seems an unreal fantasy. Eventually, like a thunderbolt, a shell pierces the ship. A deafening explosion sends lethal particles of shrapnel and flying debris ricocheting off the ship's interior panels. Unfortunate men are cut down instantly in death or mutilation. Fire, fumes and flooding in darkened confined spaces summon terror to the survivors. Exercises can never equal the real thing."

The light cruisers *Achilles* and *Ajax* moved in under the cover of smoke screens to sandwich *Graf Spee* and began firing on her from both sides, inflicting substantial damage to the German warship.

Now *Graf Spee* laid a smoke screen to cover a manoeuver turning to the west, and Langsdorff sent a signal to the German Admiralty: "I have taken fifteen hits. Food stores and galleys destroyed. I am heading for Montevideo." He believed that one or both of the enemy cruisers was about to launch a torpedo attack on his ship. Both *Ajax* and *Achilles* had suffered considerable damage in the fight thus far, but followed *Graf Spee* to Montevideo where they stationed themselves off the estuary as the German warship entered the harbour. The badly damaged *Exeter* now had only one functioning gun turret. She had suffered the loss of sixty-one dead and twenty-three wounded in the encounter.

Langsdorff asked Montevideo authorities for permission to spend the next fifteen days repairing his ship there to make her seaworthy again. He was granted just seventy-two hours. In that time his sixty wounded crewmen were treated and his thirty-six dead were removed for burial. The Royal Navy, meanwhile, sent another cruiser, HMS *Renown*, to join *Achilles*, *Ajax* and *Exeter* in the area. Langsdorff himself had been wounded twice by flying splinters while standing on the open bridge.

Due to a concentrated naval intelligence campaign by the British Admiralty in which messages were sent out on frequencies known to be monitored by German intelligence, Langsdorff was led to believe that various heavy units of the Royal Navy were in or approaching the area to threaten*Graf Spee*. He believed, incorrectly, that the British aircraft carrier *Ark Royal* had also been sent to the aid of the cruisers there, and on 16 December he sent following signal to Admiral Raeder in Berlin: "Apart from the British cruisers and destroyers, the aircraft carrier *Ark Royal* and the battlecruiser *Renown* have joined the naval forces to tightly block our escape route. No prospect of breaking out into the open sea or reaching home. Propose emerging as far as neutral waters limit and attempt to fight through to Buenos Aires using remaining ammunition. Breakout would result in certain destruction of *Graf Spee* with no chance of damaging enemy ships. Request decision whether to scuttle despite inadequate depth of water or accept internment." Raeder discussed the request with Hitler and signalled Langsdorff that the *Graf Spee* was to remain in Montevideo for as long as the authorities there would allow and that a breakout to Buenos Aires was approved, but internment in Uruguay was not, and if scuttling was necessary, everything in the ship was to be destroyed.

In assessing the damage incurred by his ship in the engagement with the British warships, he learned that the oil purification plant needed to prepare the diesel fuel for the engines, was destroyed. He found too, that *Graf Spee*'s desalination plant and kitchen were also ruined and that she had taken a heavy hit in the bow, all of which would seriously affect her seaworthiness in the heavy seas of the North Atlantic. Her repairs were still expected to take two weeks.

Unwilling to risk the lives of his crew, Langsdorff elected to scuttle *Graf Spee*. He knew that despite Uruguay being officially neutral in the war, his ship would be interned there if he overstayed the seventy-two hours he had been given to repair it and British intelligence officers would certainly be given access to it by the Uruguayan Navy. On 17 December, he ordered the destruction of all important equipment and documents aboard the ship, as well as the dispersement of her remaining ammunition in preparation for the scuttling. The next day, with he and forty other remaining crew members took *Graf Spee* into the outer roadstead.

From *Langsdorff of the Graf Spee, Prince of Honour*: "As the hours ticked away, the world waited. A blood-bath seemed certain. Tension mounted at 6:45 p.m. when a black cloud of smoke puffed out of *Graf Spee*'s funnel. Slowly, amid the rattle of heavy chains, the forward anchor rose out of black, sucking mud. Idling diesels revved into powerful life. *Graf Spee* swung round and moved slowly into the exit channel. Two battle flags waved lazily from their halyards high on the ship's masts. A makeshift steel patch on the port bow covered a large hole suffered in the previous battle. Nevertheless, the damaged warship presented a powerful, beautiful picture as she moved gracefully toward her fate."

Upwards of 20,000 people lined the shoreline, watching as charges were set for the scuttling of the pocket battleship and she sailed to a point just beyond the three-mile limit where Captain Langsdorff and the remaining crewmen were taken from her by an Argentine tug. At eight that evening three large explosions rocked and wrecked the big warship and left her burning in a huge fireball. She quickly settled into the shallow water with much of her superstructure still above it. The ruined hulk continued to burn for several days.

From *Langsdorff of the Graf Spee, Prince of Honour*: "At 10 a.m., Monday, December 18, two seagoing tugs, *Colaso* and *Gigante*, with the barge *Chiriguana* in tow, approached Buenos Aires. Close to 1,100 weary sailors crowded into every corner of the little ships. Most of the crew wore tropical whites while the officers stood out in their blue uniforms. Men overflowed onto the gunwales and clung to the rigging trying to find breathing space. Exhausted and hungry, their uniforms sweaty and crumpled, the 'shipwrecked' sailors had escaped potential disaster in Montevideo. On the black headbands of their white hats, printed in gothic gold letters, blazed the name of their ship—Panzerschiff Admiral Graf Spee."

Captain Langsdorff wrote letters to his wife and son in Germany, and to the German ambassador in Buenos Aires. In the morning of 20 December he shot himself in the head with a pistol borrowed from the German Embassy. He was found dead in his room at the Naval Arsenal in Buenos Aires, wrapped in the ensign of his ship. The burnt-out wreck of *Graf Spee* lies in the shallows off Montevideo harbour. Her foretop can still be seen on clear days.

The ruin of *AdmiralGraf Spee*, scuttled near Montevideo.

Battleship Routine

"I ate that chow for three years. We had beans Monday, Wednesday and Saturday, three times a day. We had a lot of Spam, a LOT of Spam. We had all the coffee we wanted, made in big urns. During General Quarters, there was no chow. When we were under attack, we didn't eat. When the attack was over, the first thing we had to do was clean up the guns, get rid of the hot cases and get ready for the next battle. After that, you ate when it was time for your side to eat.

"Some of that food, for a guy who came from a small town in the middle west, I couldn't eat it. It didn't even look good. But some of those guys just sloshed it down like it was good. Some of that stuff they used to make for us was streaky, watery, gooey stuff we used to call Slumgullion. It didn't even look fit to eat. I wouldn't eat it. There was no ketchup, no butter, and no ice on the table. They made their own bread ... with a lot of weevils in it. We used to hold the bread up to the light and count the bogies in it. Sometimes there would be ten or twelve dead weevils in it. And then, when there was foul weather, and the cooks couldn't cook because the sea was too rough, we used to get bologna sandwiches. I used to fill my locker up with sandwiches because I never got seasick. The chow on the ship was good when you were in port, but when you were at sea, it was ... whatever you could get. There was one time when we were at sea for sixty days and we got beans all the time because they ran out of everything.

"We used to pick up Tokyo Rose when we were standing watch at night. She played all the nice music. Glenn Miller, Benny Goodman, Tommy Dorsey, all the good songs. You're on watch at four in the morning. You can't go to sleep. You can't even sit down. You've got to stand up. One night she said: 'Today we sank the *Blue Dragon*.' The Japanese used to call our ship the *Blue Dragon*, and we'd laugh like hell. She was always saying things like, 'You know, your wife or girlfriend is out with your neighbour. She's cheating on you.' Always planting bad thoughts in your mind.

"I used to gamble and sometimes I'd win. Craps or cards. And, I'd send money home to my father because I knew that the house wasn't paid for. I said 'Pay for the house.' I didn't know how much I sent. So, when I came back from the service, he handed me a checkbook with over $3,000. In it. I said 'What's this?' He said 'That's your money. That's the money you sent your mother to pay for the house. Now this is your money ... if you want to use it to get married, go to school, or buy a car ... nothing else. You can't waste it.' So I wound up buying a car."
—Tony Iacono, USS *New Jersey*

Chief Petty Officer Robert Sambataro served aboard the USS *Missouri* as a medical corpsman during the Korean War. "Among the ships under United Nations command was HMCS *Cayuga*. I recall that they asked for medical supplies. What I didn't know then was that the medical officer was the famous imposter Ferdinand 'Fred' Demera. We both came from Lawrence, Massachusetts.

"There have been several accounts about the various careers of Demera. He took on several guises, among them zoologist, law student, teacher, and assistant prison warden. But surely his crowning achievement was that of surgeon-lieutenant aboard the *Cayuga*.

"Demera studied all the medical books on board and performed dental surgery on the captain. He also looked after the wounded that were brought aboard. How did this come about? Well, he became a friend of a New Brunswick doctor, J.S. Cyr. He stole Cyr's medical certificates and used Cyr's

A battleship sailor aboard the USS *New Jersey* in the Second World War being illustrated with a tattoo by a shipmate.

top: A Vought OS2U Kingfisher floatplane on the catapult of the USS New Jersey in the Second World War; left: Deck hands moving shells for the big guns of a WW2 battleship of the U.S. Navy.

name when applying to join the navy. The navy was eager to have him, and since there was no medical examination and no fingerprinting, he was accepted in no time flat.

"His exploits aboard the ship made great press, but the end came for Demera when Dr Cyr in New Brunswick said that he was the real Dr Cyr. Demera was given $1,000. in back pay and deported to the U.S. No charges were filed. He died in 1982, after having been ordained a Baptist minister."

"As well as the individual acquaintance of your men, you must know the 'atmosphere' of the ship. You must be close enough in touch with your ship's company to know of any feeling or rumour in the ship which may be a bad influence; for it is your job to dispel such impressions.

"That your men should know you is equally important. They must know you well enough to look upon you as the trustee of their welfare on board and in their homes. Men are proverbially shy about putting in requests to see officers, and particularly the Captain. You must make it clear to the men that not only their Divisional Officers, but you yourself will do all you can for their welfare. One of the instinctive desires in every man's mind is for security. If the sailors know that you are watching over their home security you will have gone a long way towards getting a happy ship.

"The men will also know you indirectly in the way you handle the ship and exert your influence to bring the ship to a high standard, but it is during your ship's company talks that each and every man will get to know you best. For that reason you must look upon your talks to the crew as one of the most important things you do. The first point to realise on these occasions is that you are talking to a body of men, a number of whom are quite intelligent, and that it is the intelligent ones, and not the dull ones, who are going to criticise your speech afterwards. Therefore, while talking in simple language, you must never talk down to the men. Neither imagine that you will get the best out of a crew which you never address at all.

"An intelligent man wants both information and inspiration. For this reason the Silent Skipper of last-century fiction, who in some way gained the devotion of his men by never uttering a word, will not be a success today. At the same time, a sailor does not want to be mustered on someone else's messdeck to hear a succession of vague and longwinded discourses on nothing in particular. Neither does he enjoy false heroics or 'flannel.' Like his tot, the sailor prefers his talks neat. For this reason, when you talk, do it at a convenient time when everybody will hear. Make certain, also, that you have something quite definite to say, and work out exactly how to say it beforehand. If Winston Churchill has to rehearse all his speeches, there is no reason why you should not.

"Bring in all you can about ships' movements without compromising security. If you have been in action explain all you can, giving praise where due. If you have been in any large operation, use it to give the men a wider outlook, and foster a feeling of trust and admiration in the Commander-in-Chief and other senior officers.

"Finally, when addressing a ship's company, be yourself. You cannot consistently go on being someone else for the whole commission. The sailors want to be commanded by a character, not a character sketch."
—from *YOUR SHIP, NOTES AND ADVICE TO AN OFFICER ON ASSUMING HIS FIRST COMMAND, 1944.*
[Royal Navy]

In April 1924, a woman named Madeline Blair managed to stow away aboard the USS *Arizona* when the battleship was berthed in New York City. While the ship was under way to her next port of call,

left: The USS *Louisiana* off the California coast in April 1908; bottom: HMS *Prince of Wales* in 1902; below: Battleship trainees at Great Lakes Naval Training Station, Illinois, 1918.

San Pedro, California, a scandal erupted when the stowaway was discovered. It transpired that the lady had been providing favours to the sailors who helped to conceal her presence for nearly a month. Twenty-three sailors were tried and sentenced to naval prison terms of up to ten years. Blair was transferred to a commercial vessel which returned her to New York.

The USS *Missouri*, BB-63, is the last of a line of warships called Missouri. The first of these was a steam-powered wooden side-wheeled frigate completed in 1842. She had two paddle wheels and was armed with two ten-inch guns and eight eight-inch guns. On 26 August 1843, a crewman dropped a demijohn of spirits of turpentine in a store room. A fire ignited and spread so rapidly that containment was not possible. In a few hours the burnt-out hulk sank. More than 200 of her crew were rescued by the British ship-of-the-line *Malabar*. The second *Missouri* was an iron-clad centre-wheel steam sloop of the Confederate States of America. She was launched in April 1863 and was used mainly to transport workers around the coast of Louisiana. At the end of the Civil War, she was surrendered to the U.S. Navy.

BB-11, the first warship to bear the name *Missouri*, was launched 28 December 1901 and was a 12,362-ton battleship with a complement of forty officers and 521 men. She was armed with four twelve-inch guns, sixteen six-inch guns and a variety of smaller weapons. While engaged in target practice on 13 April 1904, a flare-back from one of her guns ignited a fire causing more than a thousand pounds of gunpowder to burn. Many of the ship's spaces quickly filled with deadly gas which suffocated five officers and twenty-nine men. In December 1907, BB-11 was among sixteen white-painted battleships to pass in review before President Theodore Roosevelt at Hampton Roads, Chesapeake Bay. The Great White Fleet then departed on a celebrated fourteen-month world cruise. She later served as a training ship and, in June and July 1912, helping protect American lives at Guantanamo Bay during the Cuban Revolution. She served as a training vessel with the Atantic Fleet during the First World War, as well as transporting troops to and from France. She was scrapped in January 1922, under the terms of the Washington Naval Arms Limitation Treaty.

The final battleship *Missouri*, BB-63, was commissioned on 11 June 1944. Speaking at her launch ceremonies, Senator Harry S. Truman said: "The time is surely coming when the people of Missouri can thrill with pride as the *Missouri* and her sister ships, with batteries blazing, sail into Tokyo Bay."

"We stopped off at the Hollywood USO for some coffee and doughnuts, and chatted with some of the hostesses. One of them came up with some tickets for a TV show and we decided to go. It was the popular 'Truth of Consequences' show with Jack Bailey as MC. We got there early and got seats in the front row. As they do in these shows, they always have a sub-host come out and 'warm-up' the audience. The show was to be taped for showing an hour later. It always opened with the audience laughing it up a lot. What were they laughing at? On this particular show, it was me. In order to get the audience to laugh, the sub-host picked out a soldier and a sailor from the audience to come down to the stage. We were asked our names and where we were from, and I got a word in about being stationed on the 'Mo' and that got a round of applause. We were then asked who we thought could get dressed faster, men or women. Of course, the G.I. and I both said men. So, to prove it, the sub-host brought out two suitcases. One held women's clothes, the other one, men's. We were to see how fast we could get dressed. We each chose a suitcase. I got the women's clothes.

"Now it was a matter of timing. The show was about to begin. The announcer was getting ready when the G.I. and I got the signal to start dressing, and that was all that was needed. I attacked the suitcase and threw on some panties about six sizes too large and, with a prompt from the sub-host, I started pulling a girdle over my head. This brought howls from the audience, and that was what was being taped when the show was being introduced. The G.I. and I were shuffled under the seating area, took off the clothes we had put on and, with a well-done from the sub-host, we were both handed an envelope and escorted back to our seats. When the show was over my buddies gathered around me to find out what was in the envelope. I opened it and there were four one-dollar bills, a note and a gift certificate. The note said the four dollars was to pay the taxes for the prize on the gift certificate which was for a Zenith Transoceanic Portable radio (the envy of everyone during the 1950s). The radio could be picked up at the studio tours gift shop, which at that time was closed.

"So, we left the studio and went across the street to a bar where we asked the bartender to put the TV on for us so we could watch the show we had attended, and I bought the beer with the four dollars. When the show came on, I saw the audience laughing at the G.I. and myself, and as the camera panned around, my buddies showed up, laughing with the rest of them.

The next day we toured the beaches in the hope of seeing some stars. We enjoyed the sight of thousands of bodies in skimpy bikinis. We hit all the famous beaches and the municipal pier at Santa Monica. I also ran up to the TV studio and picked up my prize radio. I was to enjoy it but a short time as it was stolen soon after. Anyway, it was a fun and relaxing liberty."
—Herb Fahr, USS *Missouri*

The Navy had installed a square white porcelain bathtub in the captain's in-port cabin of the USS *Iowa*, for President Franklin D. Roosevelt's trip to Casablanca in November 1943. Roosevelt, crippled by polio, was unable to use standard shipboard showers. Seaman First Class Leo Sicard was assigned to push Roosevelt around and help the president. "He was a real sailor, and knew his way around", remembered Sicard, who was frightened by his responsibility, but was comforted when Roosevelt said: "I'm a human being, just the same as you."

"Life in the old Navy was no picnic. Below decks, the short battleship USS *Maryland* looked like a beehive, with over 2,000 men in the ship's company. Crewmen could not have cameras and they could not go topside. For most of the four years that I was on board the *Maryland*, crew members could only be at their living quarters, their General [combat] Quarters, or perhaps have the luxury of a pass to visit the ship's barber. On the *Maryland*, the crew slept in hammocks. They had bins for mess tables and they ate in the same compartment where they slept."
—Harold Porter, USS *Maryland*

Nineteen-year-old Seaman First Class Tony Iacono was a gun-pointer in mount four, a five-inch gun mount on the battleship USS *New Jersey* in 1944. "We used to have a gunshack on the port superstructure, for the gunner's mates on the port side. It was right next to a vent that sucked hot air out of the bowels of the ship. We used to plug that up with blankets so that the chefs would sweat. Then the chefs would come up and say, 'Hey, what's happening?' And we would trade with them. We would take the blankets out of the vent in exchange for their bringing us a tray of cake.

"Few officers on assuming command realise to what extent their personality is mirrored in the ship.

Every word which you say on the bridge is noted by the ship's company. Every word which you say in the wardroom is marked by the officers. A display of unwarranted temper on the bridge, an unjust of over-hasty reprimand, a careless piece of shiphandling, an uncloaked show of anxiety, all these incidents will be reflected by your officers and men just as the planets reflect the light of the sun. Similarly, a disregard of danger on the bridge carries courage to every corner of the ship.

"Experience in the Fleet has shown that a large number of serious offences could have been avoided if the Captain's Standing Orders, particularly those concerning rum, and the inspection of libertymen returning from leave, had been more concisely written, and more rigidly applied.

"The supply and issue of rum needs a Commanding Officer's keenest supervision. It is essential that an officer attends daily issue, and checks most carefully the supply and opening of new casks. Supply Ratings will only fall to the temptation of misappropriation or the falsifying of accounts if they know that the officers are out of touch with the situation."
—from *YOUR SHIP, NOTES AND ADVICE TO AN OFFICER ON ASSUMING HIS FIRST COMMAND, 1944.*
[Royal Navy]

"Battleship sailors, we get the big head. We're the best. In any competition with another ship, we come out on top. We work hard and the work is tedious. But when we pull into port, we look good. We know that."
—Ernest Ervin, Reidsville, North Carolina

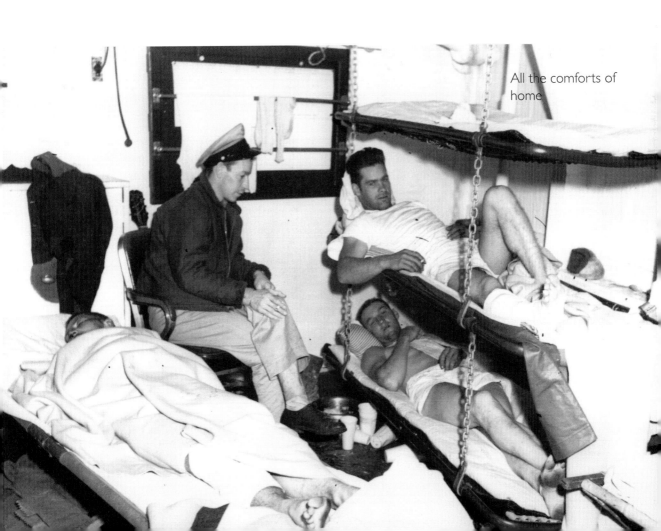

All the comforts of home.

left: Crewmen of the Imperial German Navy battleship *Grosser Kurfurst*; below: The USS *New Jersey* in New York harbour. bottom left: *Iowa*, *West Virginia* and the *Colorado* gather in Japan, October 1945.

above: An American pre-dreadnought; left: HMS Vanguard after her launching in February 1909; top right: HMS Hibernia in 1912; right: A gun pointer aboard the USS New Jersey in the Second World War, Seaman First Class Tony Iacono; far right: The USS Pennsylvania followed by a Colorado class battleship and three U.S. Navy cruisers.

The United States Atlantic Fleet steaming from Hampton Roads, Virginia in December 1907 at the start of their cruise around the world.

Big Stick

For over half a century the modern battleship was the primary capital vessel of the world's great naval powers, which were evaluated on the basis of how many of the latest battleships they operated. By the end of the Second World War, with the rise to prominence of the aeroplane, the aircraft carrier, the submarine, and the missile-firing warship, battleships were mostly withdrawn from service, scrapped or relegated to duty as memorials or museums. Those few examples that were retained for continuing service became little more than floating gun platforms for shelling enemy shore positions in subsequent conflicts.

Towards the end of the nineteenth century the battleship came into its own, generally as a relatively fast warship with a displacement in the region of 15,000 tons, and a primary armament of four twelve-inch guns augmented by a number of smaller weapons. The earliest examples of battleship fleet combat action occurred in 1898 in the Spanish-American War, when U.S. Navy battleships crushed the Spanish fleet off Cuba, and in 1905, with the Battle of Tsushima between Russia and Japan.

With the appearance of HMS *Dreadnought* in 1906, a warship heavily influenced by Tsushima, the type entered an entirely new era, that of the innovative, powerful, armoured, big-gun battleship. The great naval powers had engaged in arms races and spent many millions on the battleships of the period which, by the time of the international naval arms limitation treaties of the 1920s and 1930s, were themselves extremely limited in numbers, though not in technological development. Central to that development were moves toward vessels of greater armament and bigger guns.

In the whole history of the modern battleship, five classes stand out as the most powerful, best-armed vessels ever built. In order of most powerfully armed, they are: the Japanese *Yamato* class of the Second World War, lead ship of her class; the heaviest and most powerfully-armed battleship ever. Displacing 72,800 tons fully loaded, *Yamato* was armed with nine 18.1-inch guns which fired projectiles weighing 3,219 pounds each. A broadside salvo from her big guns weighed 28,971 pounds. They could shoot to a range of 45,960 yards or just over twenty-six miles.

Yamato was specifically designed to out-gun and out-perform the vessels of the U.S. Navy battleship fleet. Serving as the flagship of Admiral Isoroku Yamamoto, he directed Japanese fleet operations from the bridge of *Yamato* in the Battle of Midway, a resounding defeat for Japan, and the turning point in the Pacific War. *Musashi*, the sister ship of *Yamato*, took over then as flagship of the Combined Fleet. The only occasion in which *Yamato* fired her main guns at enemy surface targets was in October 1944 in the Battle of Leyte Gulf. By April 1945, the main Japanese fleet was reduced to very limited capability and depleted resources in her home islands, which left her short of fuel for many of her remaining warships. Desperate to slow or halt the Allied advance on Japan, *Yamato* was sent to Okinawa on a one-way trip to make a stand and defend the island from enemy invasion. She was under orders to fight until she was destroyed. On 7 April she was attacked and sunk by American carrier-based bombers and torpedo bombers, with the loss of the majority of her crew.

Next in line of the most powerful battleship gun platforms is the *Iowa* class of the U.S. Navy. Ordered by the navy to escort its fast carrier task forces in the Pacific theater of operations, the *Iowas* were partially based on the example of the previous *South Dakota* and *North Carolina* classes of battleships and were designed for speed and great firepower. The class comprised four ships, *Iowa, New Jersey, Missouri* and *Wisconsin* and, between the 1940s and 1990s, were involved in four major con-

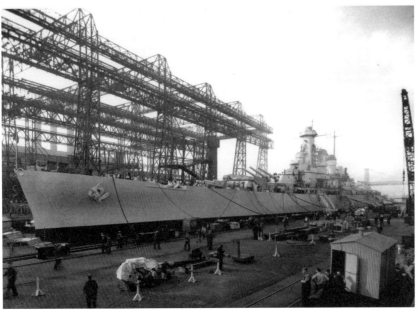

left: The batteship USS *North Carolina* nearing completion in the New York Navy Yard in 1941; above: A battleship gun crew at work in the Second World War; below: A stamp honouring HMS *Warspite*.

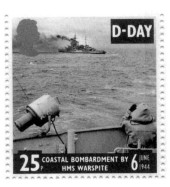

D-DAY

25 P COASTAL BOMBARDMENT BY HMS WARSPITE 6 JUNE 1944

flicts, the Korean and Vietnam wars, the Iraq war and the First Gulf War. All four were finally decommissioned by the navy in the early 1990s in conjunction with the end of the Cold War period. In the 1980s all four ships were reactivated and were rearmed with missiles in addition to their original armament of nine sixteen-inch big guns and a variety of smaller weaponry. Those big guns fired a 2,700-pound shell over a maximum range of 42,345 yards. The shell was actually superior to that of *Yamato*, with better ballistics, thus probably making the Iowa class warships at least the power equal of the great Japanese battleship. The Iowa class battleships were the subject of debate by the U.S. Congress about the role of battleships in the modern navy. In 2012, the battleship *Iowa* was the last of her class to become a non-profit maritime museum in the United States.

Named after the German Chancellor Otto von Bismarck, the battleship *Bismarck* was the lead of the two-ship class that included the *Tirpitz*. *Bismarck* was built in the Blohm und Voss shipyard at Hamburg and was launched in February 1939. She and *Tirpitz* were the largest battleships ever built in Germany. In her eight-month career under the command of Captain Ernst Lindemann, *Bismarck* undertook just one offensive operation. In company with the heavy cruiser *Prinz Eugen*, she was assigned to raid Allied shipping from North America to Britain. Discovered on several occasions by British warships and aircraft off Scandinavia, the two German vessels were subject to efforts by the Royal Navy to block their route. In the Battle of Denmark Strait, the *Bismarck* encountered, attacked and destroyed the British battlecruiser HMS *Hood* and caused HMS *Prince of Wales* to retreat. In the combat, *Bismarck* suffered three hits and a major oil leak. The loss of *Hood* led to Prime Minister Winston Churchill's determination to sink the *Bismarck* and a massive Royal Navy effort to do so as the German battleship steamed towards occupied France and relative safety. In her flight, *Bismarck* was caught and attacked by Fairey Swordfish torpedo bombers from the carrier *Ark Royal*, which struck her with a vital blow making her steering gear inoperable. The next morning, she was heavily damaged in an attack by British warships and was then scuttled. She sank with a huge loss of life.

An evolution of the French *Dunkerque* class battleships, the *Richelieu* was the lead ship of her class and was originally designed in the early 1930s to counter the Italian *Littorio* class battleships. She was the first modern French battleship to be designed and constructed following the 1922 Washington Naval Arms Limitation Treaty. She displaced 35,000 tons and her main armament was composed of eight fifteen-inch guns that fired a 1,949-pound armour-piercing projectile over a maximum distance of 45,600 yards. Her primary vulnerability was probably her insufficient anti-aircraft capability. She was fast, thirty-five mph, second only to the fast battleships of the U.S. Navy.

A controversial design feature of *Richelieu* was having all of her fifteen-inch main guns mounted forward within two big traversing turrets with each mounting four guns. The reasoning behind this decision was that it reduced the total armour weight across just two turrets, as opposed to the more common positioning of three or four turrets. An armoured divider was built between the left and right gun pairings in each turret, to minimise the potential damage to the quad turret from a direct hit. *Richelieu*'s big guns operated in pairs, unlike those on the other battleships of her time, so if one of her turrets received a direct hit, only half of the armament in it would likely be put out of action.

To evade capture by the Germans, the nearly-completed *Richelieu* departed her berth at Brest in June 1940, joining the Allied side in 1943 after a period in the hands of the Vichy French. Following a refitting in the New York Navy Yard, she operated with the Royal Navy in the Indian Ocean for the balance of the war and served thereafter with French forces in Indochina. In 1952, *Richelieu* was assigned as a gunnery training ship in Toulon. She was scrapped in the late 1960s.

below: The USS *Wisconsin* berthed at the Hampton Roads Naval Museum in Norfolk, Virginia; right: a battleship of the Royal Navy in the Second World War; bottom right: Handling sixteen-inch shells aboard the USS *New Jersey*.

After *Richelieu*, the next most powerfully armed battleship of all time was HMS *King George V*, lead ship of her class, which included *Prince of Wales, Duke of York, Howe,* and *Anson.* All five ships of the class served in the Second World War. *Prince of Wales* and *King George V* participated in the pursuit, attack and sinking of the German battleship Bismarck between 24 and 26 May 1941. While deployed off Singapore, *Prince of Wales* and the battlecruiser HMS *Repulse* were both attacked and sunk by Japanese aircraft. *Prince of Wales* was the only warship of her class to be lost in combat. In a 1943 engagement, *Duke of York* participated in the sinking of the German battleship *Scharnhorst*—the last occasion in which British and German capital ships engaged in combat during the war. *Anson* and *Howe* spent the bulk of their wartime careers on escort duty for several of the Arctic Circle convoys to and from Russia. In the Pacific war, *Howe* and *King George V* also provided off-shore bombardment against the Ryuku Islands. After the war, all the ships of the class were phased out of service and sold for scrap.

The ships of the *King George V* class were each armed with twelve fourteen-inch main guns in three quadruple turrets, whose massive weight is believed to have compromised the required amount of armour protection within the proscribed 35,000-ton displacement limitation, raising concerns about the stability of the ship. Ultimately, the second forward turret was replaced by a smaller two-gun turret, enabling improved armour protection. In wartime service the quad turrets were less reliable than had been expected. Insufficient clearance between the rotating and fixed structure of the turret, insufficient full-calibre firing exercises and an extensive arrangement to prevent flash from reaching the magazines, added to the mechanical complexity, all of which created problems for the crews in extended battle actions. Later, improvements to the clearances and the mechanical linkages, coupled with better training, resulted in greater reliability in the quad turrets.

In *The Final Action*, author John Roberts wrote: "At 0847 *Rodney* opened fire . . . at a gun range of 23,500 yards, followed by *King George V* one minute later at 24,600 yards . . . Initially she [KGV] did well achieving 1.7 salvoes per minute while employing radar control but she began to suffer severe problems from 0920 onward [Note: KGV had opened fire at 0848 and fired for about 25 minutes at 1.7 salvoes per minute until 0913, when the type 284 radar broke down, but with no recorded loss of 14-inch gun output until 0920]. KGV recorded 14 straddles out of 34 salvoes fired from 0853 to 0913 when using her type 284 radar for ranging and spotting. 'A' turret was completely out of action for 30 minutes [from 0920], after firing about 23 rounds per gun, due to a jam between the fixed and revolving structure in the shell room and 'Y' turret was out of action for 7 minutes due to drill errors . . . Both guns in 'B' turret, guns 2 and 4 in 'A' turret and gun 2 in 'Y' turret were put out of action by jams and remained so until after the action—5 guns out of 10! There were a multitude of other problems with mechanical failures and drill errors that caused delays and missed salvoes. There were also some misfires—one gun (3 of 'A' turret) misfired twice and was out of action for 30 minutes before it was considered safe to open the breech."

26 December 1943. In the early action against the *Scharnhorst* in the Battle of the North Cape, achieved thirty-one straddles out of fifty-two broadsides fired and later in the action she achieved twenty-one straddles out of twenty-five broadsides, an exceptionally fine performance. Altogether, *Duke of York* fired 450 shells in seventy-seven broadsides. The ships of the *King George V* class were the only British battleships to be mounted with fourteen-inch main guns; their planned successors—beyond treaty limitations—were to employ new sixteen-inch guns and triple mounts.

"I always wanted to be a gunner's mate, so I asked around to find out how I could get reassigned, and was told to see a turret captain. I then went to see him and he said he had to check with the

above: A gunnery mate aboard the USS *New Jersey* handling powder bags for the ship's sixteen-inch main guns in November 1944.

below: U.S. Navy reservists recruiting in New York for the First World War in 1917; left: HMS *Hood*, the pride of the Royal Navy, in 1932. The *Hood* was struck by several shells from the German battleship *Bismarck* on 24 May 1941. She exploded and sank during the Battle of the Denmark Strait.

INVEST

MEN WANTED
FOR THE
U·S·NAVY
APPLY HERE

division officer and they took me in the turret and put me to work on the number two gun. Each man there had a part of the inside of the turret to take care of and wipe down and clean and shine every day. I was a powder car man, running an electric hoist back and forth down to the upper handling room. There was nothing but powder in that room. It was directly under the projectile room where the shells were kept. We all trained so that we knew every job around the turret."
—Richard McCutcheon, USS *West Virginia*

"We were loading ammo and I was standing near a vestibule on the powderflats as a high-explosive round was being lowered. I was on the sound-powered phones with the guy who was lowering the round from the main deck. I told him to stop lowering the round, which weighed 2,700 pounds, but it kept coming down. I yelled into the phones to stop, but the round just kept on coming. I tried to squeeze into the vestibule. I was cornered, with nowhere to go as the projectile kept coming toward me. Then, just as it was about to pin me against the bulkhead, the tip of the projectile warhead caught on a half-inch pipe and came to rest about four inches from my hip. You can imagine the relief I felt."
—Mike Holloman, USS *Missouri*

"Do battleships move sideways when they fire their big guns? What looks like a side-ways wake is just the water being boiled up by the muzzle blasts. The ship doesn't move an inch or even heel from a broadside. The guns have a recoil slide of up to forty-eight inches and the shock is distributed evenly through the turret foundation and the hull structure. The mass of a 57,000-ton ship is just too great for the recoil of the guns to move it. But because of the expansion range of the overpressure (muzzle blast), a lot of the rapidly displaced air presses against the bulkheads and decks. Those structures that are not armored actually flex inwards just a bit, thus displacing air quickly inside the ship and causing loose items to fly around, sort of like having your house sealed up with all windows and vents closed and when you slam the front door quickly, the displaced air pops open the kitchen cabinets."
—R.A. Landgraff

far left: HMS *Royal Oak*, a *Revenge* class Royal Navy battleship which was sunk on 14 October 1939 by the German submarine *U-47* at Scapa Flow. 833 seamen were lost in *Royal Oak*, Günther Prien, in command of the *U-47*, was awarded the Knight's Cross of the Iron Cross, for the action; left: The USS *Mississippi* served in the Pacific campaign of the Second World War and in the Battle of Surigao Strait, the last battleship engagement in history.

In the Second World War, the aircraft carrier replaced the battleship as the capital ship of the great navies. Here the Royal Navy carrier *Illustrious* is dwarfed by the American Nimitz class carrier *John C. Stennis*.

The New Capital Ship

The term capital ship refers to the most significant, most important and most heavily armed and armoured warship in a naval fleet. These are normally the largest vessels of the fleet, projecting the greatest power and in the lead of the fleet. In the modern era, the all-steel battleship held sole possession of that role for much of the last half of the nineteenth, and most of the first half of the twentieth centuries. Then, in the midst of the Second World War, the relatively sudden rise and dominance of naval aviation and air power, coupled with the evolution and enormous capability of the aircraft carrier, led almost overnight to a sea change in that critical role. Suddenly, the primary power criteria, the new measure of a navy's strength, influence, and overall capability, was seen not so much in terms of tonnage or gun diameters, but rather in the mobility and flexibility to bring one or more large sea-air striking forces capable of large-scale aerial attack with bombs, torpedoes and other weapons, to within strike distance of a conflict or threat, anywhere in the world. The immensely powerful, highly-capable aircraft carrier has, as exemplified by the fleets of the United States Navy, developed into a particularly formidable force of carrier battle groups. In recent years these have evolved into what are now called carrier strike groups, each comprising a truly enormous 'mother ship' which, in the example of the U.S. Navy, is presently a *Nimitz* class carrier.

Prior to the adoption of all-steel battleships late in the nineteenths century, the Royal Navy applied a rating system to classify a ship-of-the-line. A ship considered a First Rate typically carried at least 100 guns which were positioned on three or four decks. A ship categorized as Second Rate had ninety to ninety-eight guns. Third Rate identified a ship armed with sixty-four to eighty guns, and Fourth Rate applied to a ship carrying forty-six to sixty guns, though vessels of this last category were usually not considered of sufficient power to fight in a line of battle and were generally relegated to lesser duties. The lowest ranks were: Fifth Rate which were frigates, and Sixth Rate, made up of small frigates and corvettes.

With the international naval arms limitation treaties of Washington and London in the 1920s and 1930s, the term capital ship came to apply to the battleships of the new dreadnought type. Battleships and battlecruisers were from that point the typical capital ships of the world's great navies, through the early years of the Second World War. The characteristics they generally shared were a displacement in the region of 20,000 tons or more, heavy armour protection, and large-calibre guns. An exception was the German *Deutschland* class very heavy cruiser, widely recognized as a capital ship, and referred to by the British as a pocket battleship, as were the *Alaska* class cruisers of the U.S. Navy in the Second World War.

After the Japanese attack on the American battleships at Pearl Harbor on 7 December 1941, the United States had to turn to its aircraft carriers in the Pacific and that reliance certainly contributed to the U.S. Navy's transition from the battleship to the carrier as its new capital ship. That transition would lead eventually to absolute American supremacy in fleet supercarriers and their strike groups. With ten *Nimitz* class nuclear-powered supercarriers, each displacing a staggering 102,000 tons and accommodating eighty-five fixed-wing and rotary aircraft, the U.S. Navy operates what is probably the most formidable threat ever deployed. The currently active *Nimitz* class carriers deployed were built by the Newport News Shipbuilding Company in Virginia. They are: USS *Nimitz* (CVN-68), USS *Dwight D. Eisenhower* (CVN-69), USS *Carl Vinson* (CVN-70), USS *Theodore Roosevelt* (CVN-71), USS

HMS *Glorious*

HMS *Indomitable*

HMS *Argus*

HMS *Ark Royal*

HMS *Eagle*

Abraham Lincoln (CVN-72), USS *George Washington* (CVN-73), USS *John C. Stennis* (CVN-74), USS *Harry S. Truman* (CVN-75), USS *Ronald Reagan* (CVN-76), and USS *George H. W. Bush* (CVN-77). With a length of 1,092 feet, a beam of 252 feet, and a draught of thirty-seven feet, they are capable of a thirty-five mph top speed and have an unlimited range over a period of twenty to twenty-five years unrefueled. Each is manned by a ship's company of 3,200 personnel and an Air Wing of 2,480 personnel. They are equipped with four steam catapults for launching fixed-wing aircraft.

The USS *Nimitz*, first ship of its class, was named after WW2 Pacific Fleet commander Admiral Chester W. Nimitz, the Navy's last Fleet Admiral. The *Nimitz* was commissioned on 3 May 1975. The USS *George H. W. Bush* is the tenth and last ship of its class and was commissioned on 10 January 2009. With the retirement of the Navy's F-14 Tomcat fighter in September 2006, the current Air Wings flying from the *Nimitz* class carriers are primarily made up of F/A-18E/F Super Hornets and F/A-18 Hornets. Additional ship protection is provided by short-range defensive weapons that include Sea Sparrow and Phalanx missiles.

Two new-class supercarriers are currently under construction. The USS *Gerald R. Ford* (CVN-78), lead ship of its class, is expected to be launched in 2013. It will replace the USS *Enterprise* (CVN-65), the U.S. Navy's first nuclear-powered carrier, which was decommissioned in December 2012. The USS *John F. Kennedy* (CVN-79), will be the second *Ford* class carrier. The Navy plans to gradually replace all of the Nimitz class carriers, one for one, every five to six years, with the new Ford class ships which will be the largest warships ever built. These new and improved capital ships will enable the U.S. Navy to continue to project American power and protect the sea lanes through the twenty-first century. Each of the new Ford class carriers will have an embarked Air Wing of eighty-five to ninety fixed-wing,

HMS *Ocean*

HMS *Courageous*

rotary, VSTOL and unmanned aerial vehicle aircraft, a strike force greater than that of most existing air forces.

Improvements in the *Ford* class carriers will include a more efficient nuclear reactor system providing much more power than that of the *Nimitz* class ships; new electromagnetic aircraft launch and recovery systems to replace the current steam catapults and arrestor systems; a redesigned, more efficient island structure; more automated systems reducing the manpower requirement overall, more efficient aircraft weapons handling, battle management and damage control operations; improved electrical power; and greater operating capability for both the Air Wing and the carrier itself.

The warships of the *Nimitz* class were designed in support of the U.S. military during the Cold War and included the use of nuclear power instead of oil for greater endurance when on lengthy, high-seas deployment. They were designed with greater flexibility to adjust their weapons systems based on new technological and intelligence developments. At the beginning of the programme, they were called attack carriers, however, the *Nimitz* carriers since the *Carl Vinson* have been built with anti-submarine capabilities, enabling them to operate in a wider range of activity, including air and sea blockades, mine laying, and missile strikes on land, air and sea targets.

With a total construction cost of about $4.5 billion, each ship of the *Nimitz* class since the *Theodore Roosevelt* has been built using modular construction techniques. The *George H.W. Bush*, for example, was assembled from 161 modules, massive sections that were welded together, their electrical and plumbing equipment already fitted for greatly improved efficiency of construction, and giant gantry cranes lifted the modules into the dry dock for final assembly.

Each of the carriers of the *Nimitz* class is powered by two Westinghouse A4W nuclear reactors

far left: A Royal Navy Swordfish crew and their aircraft; left: The U.S. Navy carrier *Badoeng Strait* with F4U Corsair fighters on deck; centre left: Lt JG William Adams reports after a dive-bombing mission to New Guinea, April 1944; centre right: An F6FHellcat launches; bottom left: A landing signal officer on the USS *Enterprise* in WW2; bottom right: A Curtiss SB2C Helldiver aboard the USS *Bunker Hill* in 1944.

which are housed in separate compartments. With a maximum power production of 260,000 bhp (190 MW), the reactors heat water through nuclear fission. The hot water then passes through four General Electric turbines which power the four twenty-five-foot diameter bronze propellers, each weighing about thirty tons. The nuclear-powered *Nimitz* class carriers can operated for more than twenty years without refueling. Their predicted service life is fifty years.

The *Nimitz* carriers are protected by the aircraft of their Air Wings, but also carry defensive systems for use against hostile aircraft and missiles. These include the NATO RIM-7 Sea Sparrow missile and the 20mm Phalanx missile defense cannon. An exception is the *Ronald Reagan* which uses the RIM-116 Rolling Airframe Missile system, which has since also been installed on the *Nimitz* and the *George Washington*, and will ultimately be installed on the other carriers of the class as they receive their Refueling Complex Overhauls. For armour protection, the carriers since the *Theodore Roosevelt* have been built with 2.5-inch Kevlar over their vital spaces. The *Nimitz, Eisenhower,* and *Vinson* have been retrofitted with the Kevlar armour as well. The *Nimitz* carriers are equipped with various countermeasures including MK36 decoy launchers which deploy infrared flares and chaff to disrupt the sensors of incoming missiles; as well as a torpedo defense system and a torpedo countermeasures system. Additionally, they carry electronic warfare systems to detect and disrupt hostile radar signals.

When a *Nimitz* class carrier deploys to sea, it embarks one of ten Carrier Air Wings. It can accommodate up to 130 F/A-18 Hornets, but is normally equipped with eighty-five to ninety aircraft of various types. The Air Wing is integrated into the specific assignment of the carrier deployment, but the pilots and aircrews, the maintenance, aircraft and ordnance handling, and the emergency procedures Air Wing personnel operate as a separate entity from the ship's crew. Typically, a carrier Air Wing may be made up of twelve to fourteen F/A-18E or F Super Hornet strike fighters; two squadrons of ten

left: The Royal Navy escort carrier HMS *Pursuer*, an American-built ship in the British WW2 inventory; top left:: Deck handlers respotting an aircraft; top right: A U.S. Navy Vought F4U Corsair fighter; right: Grumman F6F Hellcats run up their engines before launching from the USS *Bunker Hill* in 1944.

to twelve F/A-18C Hornet strike fighters (one squadron of which is often provided by the United States Marine Corps; four to six EA-6B Prowlers for electronic warfare; four to six E-2C Hawkeyes for airborne early warning; C-2 Greyhounds for logistics; and a helicopter squadron of six to eight SH-60F and HH-60H Seahawks for anti-submarine work.

With the flight deck angled at nine degrees, aircraft can be launched from the ship's four steam catapults, while other aircraft are being recovered simultaneously using the four arrestor wires crossing the deck. *Reagan* and *Bush*, the two newest carriers of the class, are fitted with three arrestor wires rather than four, as the fourth was so rarely used that it was thought to be unnecessary. All the aircraft operations of the Air Wing are controlled from the bridge of the carrier by the air boss. Aircraft are moved between the hangar deck and the flight deck by four large elevators and the three hangar bays of the hangar deck are separated by thick steel doors intended to restrict the spread of fire between the bays.

In deployment, the carrier is the lead ship of a powerful Strike Group of several warships and supply vessels. The short-range defensive armament of the carrier itself is designed to be a last line of defence against enemy aircraft and missiles. The carrier is further protected by the other warships of the Strike Group which are armed with Tomahawk missiles and the Aegis Combat System to guard the carrier from attack. In addition to the carrier, the Strike Group typically contains as many as six surface vessels including frigates, guided missile cruisers, and guided missile destroyers, for anti-aircraft and anti-submarine warfare; one or two attack submarines for locating and destroying enemy surface ships and submarines, and ammunition, oiler, and supply ships for replenishment.

It has often been said the flight deck of an aircraft carrier during flight operations may be the most

top far left: A Japanese suicide plane aimed for the USS *Sangamon,* but missed; top left: U.S. Navy Fleet Admiral Chester W. Nimitz; far left: The pilots of a U.S. Navy fighter squadron aboard the carrier *Lexington* celebrate the downing of seventeen enemy aircraft off the island of Tarawa on 23 November 1943; left: Morris Montgomery and his granddaughter, Shannon Callahan, a Naval Flight Officer. He served on the escort carrier USS *Gambier Bay* when it was attacked and sunk by cruisers and battleships of the Imperial Japanese Navy in the Battle of Leyte Gulf, 25 October 1944.

U.S. Navy flight deck crewmen on the attack carriers off Vietnam often worked eighteen-hour days and had to be able to catch a quick nap when they could during a lull in operations.

dangerous environment there is. In combat conditions deadly incidents and injuries are to be expected and have always been part of the deal on carriers. And under conditions in which exercises, training flights, and combat operations are being conducted, frequently on a round-the-clock basis, a number accidents, incidents, crashes, and fires are virtually inevitable. An example occurred on 26 May 1981, with the crash of an EA-6B Prowler on the flight deck of the carrier *Nimitz*. Fourteen ship's crew members were killed and forty-five were injured. Forensic testing following the crash, and the investigation findings led to mandatory drug testing of all service personnel.

In another notable incident, aboard the carrier *Abraham Lincoln* in 1994, Lt. Kara Hultgreen, the Navy's first female F-14 Tomcat pilot, was killed in an attempted landing during a training exercise.

The threat of deadly fire on board an aircraft carrier became reality in May 2008 as the *George Washington* was being transferred to her current home port at Yokosuka, Japan. A serious fire broke out in which thirty-seven sailors were injured and the repair bill came to seventy million dollars. The cause was unauthorized smoking near improperly stored flammable refrigerant.

Commissioned in May 1975, the USS *Nimitz*, in one of the earliest operations she took part in, initiated Operation Eagle Claw in 1980 when she was sent to the Indian Ocean after hostages were taken in the U.S. Embassy in Tehran. In company with the USS *Forrestal* in August 1981, *Nimitz* conducted a Freedom of Navigation exercise in the Gulf of Sidra, near Libya. In that exercise, two of her F-14 Tomcats shot down two Libyan aircraft in what has become known as the Gulf of Sidra incident.

In two significant assignments for carriers of the *Nimitz* class during the 1990s, all the active ships in the class were involved in the Gulf War, and Operation Southern Watch which continued into 2003. In Operations Desert Storm and Desert Shield, only the *Theodore Roosevelt* was active in a combat role during these operations. During the Gulf War period, the *Lincoln* was diverted from her mission, to the Indian Ocean; the eruption of Mount Pinatubo in the Philippines requiring her assistance in the evacuation of civilians from the island of Luzon in Operation Fiery Vigil, and following that she was sent to Somalia to participate in United Nations humanitarian operations in which her aircraft flew patrols over the Mogadishu area for four weeks. After that, *Lincoln* took part in Operation Vigilant Sentinel in the Persian Gulf. In 1991, the *Theodore Roosevelt* aircraft flew patrols in support of the Kurds over northern Iraq in Operation Provide Comfort in 1991. In 1996, the *George Washington* took part in Operation Decisive Endeavor in Bosnia and Herzegovina.

In her first deployment after commissioning, the *Harry S. Truman*'s Air Wing flew 869 sorties in Operation Southern Watch, which included air strikes against Iraqi air defence sites following Iraqi surface-to-air missile attacks on United Nations coalition forces. With the terrorist attacks on New York and Washington of 11 September 2001, the *Carl Vinson* and *Theodore Roosevelt* participated in Operation Enduring Freedom in the Afghanistan area. The *Vinson* launched the first air strikes of the operation on 7 October 2001. Meanwhile, the *George Washington* and the *John C. Stennis* carried out homeland security operations off the U.S. west coast. In the period since, all the active carriers of the *Nimitz* class have operated in the Iraq and Afghanistan regions. The carriers have also provided considerable support and assistance aid following natural disasters including the December 2004 tsunami in Indonesia, in which the *Lincoln* took part; the involvement of the *Truman* in aid after Hurricane Katrina in 2005; the *Reagan* in the Philippines following Typhoon Fengshen in 2008; and the *Vinson* off Haiti after the devastating earthquake there in 2010.

The value and importance of the modern aircraft carrier is not limited to her role as a travelling air base in conflict situations, nor as a big-stick deterrent. She has come to be seen as a powerful

left: Accidents happen, like this one in which a Grumman TBM-3 Avenger torpedo bomber ripped up the flight deck of the USS *Philippine Sea*. right: The Plymouth, England, Naval War Memorial; right centre: The Air Boss controls all flight operations of the carrier Air Wing; bottom right: A naval aviator suits up for a mission in the 1970s.

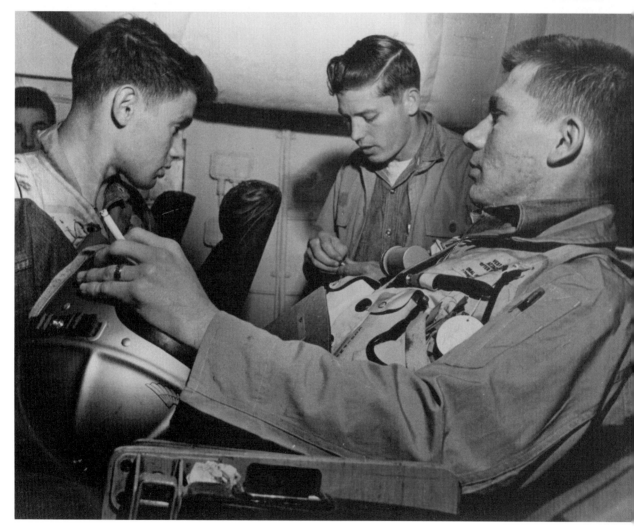

diplomatic tool in developing and enhancing relations with allies and potential allies. Such relations can be and are frequently advanced when a giant *Nimitz* class carrier visits a country and senior officers of that country's navy are invited aboard to observe operating activities, interact with the carrier's officers, or participate as part of an international task force. These visits can occur in ordinary training situations or in actual combat operations.

In a move calculated to boost civilian morale in the United States, as well as to begin to pay the Japanese back for their raid on Pearl Harbor, the U.S. Army Air Force planned and carried out a bold bombing attack on Tokyo in the spring of 1942. Led by Lieutenant Colonel James Doolittle, a force of sixteen B-25 Mitchell bombers took off from the flight deck of the carrier USS *Hornet* on the morning of 18 April. They flew 550 miles west to bomb various targets in the Japanese capital city. While the damage done was relatively small, the point had been made. It was a tiny taste of the whirlwind Japan would reap before she would finally be forced to surrender in the summer of 1945.

And now I see with eye serene / The very pulse of the machine; A traveller between life and death; the reason firm, the temperate will, / Endurance, foresight, strength and skill; A perfect Woman, nobly planned, / To warn, to comfort, and command; And yet a spirit still, and bright / With something of angelic light.
—from *She Was a Phantom of Delight*, by William Wordsworth

Rear Admiral Heijiro Abe, Imperial Japanese Navy (Ret.), retained a souvenir of his visit to Pearl Harbor on 7 December 1941, a yellowing photograph he had taken from his Nakajima bomber as the squadron he commanded dropped their armour-piercing bombs on the vessels in battleship row. On his first run over the harbour, Abe encountered heavy smoke from an earlier attack by Japanese torpedo bombers. The smoke obscured his target, the USS *West Virginia*, forcing him to lead the squadron around for a second run. When he released his single bomb he watched it strike what he believed must have been the ship's powder magazine. He recalled seeing the great ship shake convulsively and belch flames from many openings. He recorded that instant with his German-made camera and returned to his carrier where he had four prints of the photo made—one for the carrier task force chief, one for the skipper of the ship, one for Imperial Headquarters in Tokyo, and one for himself. His print is the only one known to have survived the war. He has guarded the photo carefully over the years. His greatest wish had been to one day return to Pearl Harbor "to offer prayers for the repose of the souls of the fallen Americans there. I have to do it before I die."

top left: 801 Squadron Fleet Air Arm Sea Harrier pilot Peter Wilson; centre top: U.S. Naval Flight Officer Shannon Callahan trained at NAS Pensacola; far left: In a ready room of an American escort carrier in the 1950s.

The Warspite

In the long and distinguished history of the British Royal Navy, nine of its warships have been called *Warspite*. The spelling of the name has evolved, from Elizabethan times, when it was *Warspight*, to *Wastspight*, to *Warspitt*, and finally *Warspite*. With an armament of thirty-six guns, the *Warspite* of the Elizabethan privateer Sir Walter Raleigh was launched in 1596 on the Thames and displaced 650 tons. In early June of that year Raleigh set out from Plymouth in *Warspite* in the lead of one squadron of a large force of British and Dutch warships to attack their Spanish enemy's fleet of warships in the harbour of Cadiz. In doing so, he hoped to destroy Spain's increasing threat to England. The Flagship of the Royal Navy fleet was *Repulse*, in the command of the Earl of Essex, an avowed enemy of Raleigh whom he had displaced in the Queen's affections.

As the Anglo-Dutch force neared Cadiz, Raleigh's squadron was assigned to deal with any Spanish warships that might resist their approach to the harbour. When Raleigh realized that some of the other ships of Essex's fleet were putting hundreds of troops ashore to launch a direct assault on the city, he was angered, believing that in the chaos surrounding that assault, the Spanish ships might well escape, ruining the mission.

The actual overall command of the British fleet was, by order of the Queen, shared between Essex and Lord Howard of Effingham. Raleigh somehow persuaded Essex and Effingham to cease the assault on Cadiz. The co-commanders agreed to appoint Raleigh to lead an attack on Cadiz from *Warspite*. Early the next morning *Warspite* entered the harbour and received a massively hostile response from the Spanish warships there and from the local fortifications. The encounter caused severe damage to *Warspite* and the other British vessels. Although wounded himself in the battle, Raleigh remained confident and determined that his force would win the day and capture the Spanish treasure galleons which he knew to be in the harbour. Essex and Effingham, however, chose to plunder Cadiz itself instead of conforming to Raleigh's insistence that they concentrate their efforts and resources on the treasure galleons. To keep the British and Dutch invaders from taking the treasure, the Spaniards set fire to the galleons, but not before the British managed to capture twenty of them along with nearly 1,000 cannon before making their withdrawal to Plymouth.

The eighth Royal Navy warship to bear the name *Warspite* was so-named in 1912 when names were given to the new *Queen Elizabeth* class of super-dreadnought battleships which, in addition to *Warspite* and *Queen Elizabeth*, included *Barham, Malaya,* and *Valiant.* Thirty-seven-year-old First Lord of the Admiralty, Winston Churchill was bent on establishing and maintaining dominance and superiority for the Royal Navy fleet over that of the Germans. In seeking the support of the House of Commons for the new class of super-dreadnoughts, Churchill spoke to the members of Parliament about the armour of the new ships, up to thirteen-inches thick and providing a new standard of protection, as well as the huge fifteen-inch main guns and the powerful secondary six-inch guns, all of it vastly superior to what the Germans had. He referred to the new oil-burning boilers and the great speed they would provide, which he described as essential. Essential too, as he saw it, was the new ship's ability to "curl around the head of the enemy's line and concentrate awesome firepower, shattering those vessels and throwing all the ships behind them into disarray." All the current arguments favoured oil-fueled power for the new ships instead of the traditional coal. Too, an oil-powered vessel could more easily be kept stable by pumping the oil from tank to tank for optimum ballasting. Also, an oil-fueled ship could be quickly refueled at sea, elimininating the time and inconvenience of a port call at a coaling station. Churchill wrote in *The World Crisis*: " As a coal ship used up her coal, increasingly large numbers of men had to be taken, if necessary from the guns, to shovel the coal from remote and inconvenient bunkers to bunkers nearer the furnaces themselves, thus weakening the fighting efficiency of the ship perhaps at the most critical moment in the battle." Thus, the advantages of oil-fired power over that of coal were obvious. Coaling a ship took far longer and required much more manpower. A full load of coal also weighed more than a full load of oil. In saving weight, oil allowed for the use of bigger guns and more room for other facilities, including additional boilers, which brought greater speed, as well as other improvements, not least being better crew facilities.

In terms of performance, the Navy evaluated the comparative speed capability of coal-fired and oil-fired versions of the new battleship and concluded that a coal-fired version could not propel the vessel at a speed approaching the twenty-five-knot requirement established for it. Churchill was absolutely committed to oil-fired power for the new ships, in opposition to many in Britain and the British government who percieved the change from coal-fired to oil-fired warships for the Royal Navy as both unpatriotic and an insult to the British coal miner, as well as a senseless rejection of an abundant British natural resource, in favour of one that came from a foreign and as such, vulnerable source. But, with the support of the former First Sea Lord, Admiral Sir John Fisher, Churchill was able to persuade Parliament to approve the oil-burning super-dreadnought programme. In his pursuit of that programme, Churchill was gambling not only on the change to oil-burning for the new battleships, but also to the new and untested fifteen-inch main guns in his effort to gain and hold the advantage over the fleet of Germany. From *The World Crisis*: "No such thing as a modern 15-inch gun existed. None had ever been made. The advance to the 13.5-inch had in itself been a great stride. Its power was greater; its accuracy was greater; its life was much longer. Could the British designers repeat this triumph on a still larger scale and in a still more intense form?" That gamble might well have cost Churchill his career and left the British nation mostly unprepared and ill-equipped for the coming war with Germany, her well-prepared naval adversary.

In October 1912, the keels of *Queen Elizabeth* and *Warspite* were laid, and in the following year, work began on *Barham, Malaya,* and *Valiant. Warspite* was to serve in both world wars and earned more battle honours than any other ship in the history of the Royal Navy. By early in 1915, *Warspite* had been completed and fitted out, and by May her working-up exercises had been completed at Scapa Flow in the Orkneys. She was built with a displacement of 33,410 tons. She was 639 feet five inches long, with a beam of ninety feet six inches, and a draught of thirty feet six inches. She had a top speed of twenty-four knots, a range of 8,600 nautical miles at 12.5 knots, and was manned by a ship's complement of 925 to 1,220 personnel. She was armed with eight fifteen-inch guns, fourteen six-inch guns, two three-inch anti-aircraft guns, four three-pounder guns, and four twenty-one-inch torpedo tubes. By late June she had become a part of the Grand Fleet and was involved in a series of North Sea sweeps before entering the war with Germany which had begun the year before. Soon all five ships of the *Queen Elizableth* class of super dreadnoughts had finished their work-ups and been formed into the navy's new fast battleship unit, the Fifth Battle Squadron, a force mounting forty huge fifteen-inch guns.

In the evening of 30 May, *Warspite* sailed from Rosyth and met up with vessels of the Grand Fleet to participate in the Battle of Jutland. Commander Humphrey T. Walwyn, Executive Officer of *War-*

HMS *Warspite* in drydock at Rosyth for the repair of damage to her stern, received in the Jutland battle of May 31–June 1 1916.

spite: "I realised that there was something serious doing. I passed the word round to everybody that we were in for the real thing and went round all the mess-decks, and lit all Action candles, etc. Saw all doors and everything closed, and went up on deck; they were just finishing washing down the weather decks. I sent all hands away to their stations and went up to the bridge to report everything ready. There was nothing in sight except our own ships, but we were steaming hard. Hoisted Battle Ensigns and Union Jack at after struts and masthead. Went to my action station, B turret … it was now about four o'clock … got orders to load and train on Red 20°, i.e. 20° on port bow. Could not see anything at all, hazy and a lot of smoke about … I made out five columns of smoke in the mist and that was all I could see—no masts or anything else."

Now all the main warships of both the British and German fleets were sailing to the southeast and the Germans appeared to have the advantage. Their gunnery was on target. HMS *Indefatigable* was being severely damaged, along with *Lion*, the flagship of the Admiral of the Fleet, Sir David Beatty. Quite soon after that, *Indefatigable* blew up and sank.

While steaming behind Indefatigable, the super-dreadnoughts of the Fifth Battle Squadron were some 23,000 yards from their targets when the big main guns of *Warspite* opened fire on one of the German light cruisers. Commander Walwyn: "We were turning fast to starboard and as we came round eight points, or ninety degrees, I saw five enemy battlecruisers on the port bow. They were steaming the same way as we were and going very hard. I could only see their masts and the tops of their funnels above the horizon. We opened fire on number five, the *Von der Tann*, which had just destroyed the *Indefatigable*; range, I think, 23,000 yards. I distinctly saw one salvo hit. She turned away in a cloud of black and white smoke, and we turned our attention to number four, the *Moltke*." German Vizeadmiral Reinhard Scheer: ". . . superiority in firing and tactical advantages of position were decidedly on our side until 4.19 p.m., when a new unit of four or five ships of the *Queen Elizabeth* type, with a considerable surplus of speed, drew up from a northwesterly direction and . . . joined in the fighting. It was the English Fifth Battle Squadron. This made the situation critical for our battle cruisers. The new enemy fired with extraordinary rapidity and accuracy …"

In the action that followed before 5 p.m., all five of the British super-dreadnoughts were hit repeatedly by intensive gunfire from the German battlecruisers. *Malaya* and *Barham* got the worst of it, and *Warspite* too was under severe attack, but was giving as good as she got. Commander Walwyn: "I distinctly saw two of our salvoes hit the leading German battleship. Sheets of yellow flame went right over her mastheads, and she looked red fore and aft like a burning haystack. I know we hit her hard. B turret machinery working like a clockwork mouse, no hang-up of any sort whatever." But *Warspite* was now taking some extremely hard hits and one round passed right through the mess-decks and the side armour. "It burst in a terrific sheet of golden flame, stink, and impenetrable dust. Another hit below in the side aft and began to flood the steering compartment. Yet another burst in the captain's lobby, reducing it to a state of indescribable wreckage. Farther forward, X turret was hit, and water was flooding through a hole in the side, and going down the engine room air supply trunk. Another took away the engineer's office." In the next ninety minutes the fire and damage control parties put up a life-and-death struggle to stabilize and repair *Warspite* and somehow get her back in the fight. *Warspite* and *Malaya* then reengaged in fierce combat with elements of the German High Seas Fleet.

In the action, *Warspite* sustained such heavy damage that she nearly foundered, and, while attempting to avoid her sister ship *Valiant*, her steering jammed and her captain chose to maintain course, effectively running her in a circle, rather than coming to a halt. His decision resulted in her becoming even more of a target to German battlecruisers intent on finishing her off. But that, in fact, diverted German attention somewhat from the badly-damaged *Warrior*, whose crew later expressed their admiration for *Warspite*'s act, believing it had been a deliberate attempt to save them.

The *Warspite* crew regained control of her at the end of two full circles, but they emerged on a direct course for the enemy fleet. Her rangefinders and transmission station were no longer functioning and only A turret could fire, but under local control only, and its salvoes were falling short of their target. In such a condition, *Warspite* was ordered to halt for making essential repairs. For the rest of her service life she would suffer steering irregularities.

In the Battle of Jutland, fourteen members of the *Warspite* crew were killed, with sixteen wounded. One of the wounded, Warrant Officer Walter Yeo, became one of the first men to receive facial reconstruction plastic surgery. Admiral Hugh Evan-Thomas, commander of the Fifth Battle Squadron, ordered *Warspite* back to Rosyth for major repairs and while under way to her home port, she was attacked by a German U-boat which fired three torpedoes at her, all of which missed. Later, she encountered and tried to ram a surfaced U-boat. She successfully reached Rosyth and was fully repaired.

Repaired and refitted, HMS *Warspite* went in company with 220 Royal Navy warships, six American battleships, and three French warships to take the surrender of the ten German battleships and five battlecruisers in the Firth of Forth. With the end of the war, there occurred a massive cull of the main striking force of the Royal Navy. Of the key warships, only *Warspite* and her sister ships, and the five *Royal Sovereigns*, survived it and went on to take part in several annual Mediterranean cruises as part of the Atlantic Fleet.

A series of misfortunes followed *Warspite* in the last years of the First World War and after. A collision with sister ship *Valiant* on 24 August 1916 led her to repairs that lasted nearly a month. In June of the following year she was again involved in a collision, this time with HMS *Destroyer*, and in July she was damaged while at anchorage in Scapa Flow when the nearby *St Vincent* class battleship *Vanguard* exploded with the loss of hundreds in her crew when an ammunition magazine detonated. In November 1918, the last month of the war, *Warspite* was among the Royal Navy warships that sailed to Scapa Flow to receive the vessels of the German High Seas Fleet after the signing of the Armistice.

In 1924, *Warspite* was given a modernisation that would change the appearance of her superstructure. Her armour protection was improved and her armament was supplemented with additional small-calibre guns. She was again modernised and refitted in a major project carried out at Portsmouth between 1934 and 1937, in which her propulsion machinery was replaced and six individual boiler rooms were installed, in addition to other improvements that increased her fuel efficiency and reduced her fuel consumption. 1,100 tons of added armour were applied, including coverage for the boiler rooms. Four twin four-inch guns and four two-pounder pom-poms were added for anti-aircraft defence. The main gun turrets were altered to increase the elevation of the guns, giving them a further 6,000 yards of range to a maximum of 32,000 yards. Her deck armour was increased to five inches over the magazines and 3.5-inches over the machinery. With the changes to her superstructure, an aircraft hangar was fitted. The modernisation programme also included the anti-aircraft fire control system and the surface fire control system for the main guns. Following the reconstruction programme, HMS *Warspite* was recommissioned to be the flagship of the Mediterranen Fleet, commanded by Captain Victor Crutchley. But in that role, and for much of the rest of her career at sea, she continued to be plagued with steering and propulsion machinery problems, a legacy of the original damage incurred in the Battle of Jutland.

Between June 1939 and early 1940, *Warspite* went after German capital ships as a part of the Home Fleet. In April, she supported the Norwegian Campaign by attacking German shore batteries and warships in the Second Battle of Narvik. Now fitted with her own little aircraft hangar and equipped with a Fairey Swordfish torpedo bomber, the Swordfish crew located, attacked and sank the German submarine *U-64*, in the first instance of an aircraft sinking a U-boat in the war. In the battle itself, *Warspite* gun crews destroyed or heavily damaged three enemy destroyers. Later that summer, she was transferred again to the Mediterranean where she performed effectively in the Battle of Calabria, scoring an extremely accurate gunnery hit on the Italian warship *Giulio Cesare* at the remarkable distance of 26,000 yards.

On 27 March 1941, while the flagship of Admiral of the Fleet Andrew Cunningham, *Warspite* sailed out of Alexandria harbour in company with other British capital ships, having been told of the presence of an Italian battle fleet in the area. The engagement that followed was the Battle of Cape Matapan in which *Warspite* and her sister ships *Barham*, and *Valiant* made radar contact with the enemy heavy cruisers *Zara* and *Fiume*, which they promptly destroyed. A further heavy cruiser, the *Pola*, was wrecked by British torpedoes and two destroyers were sunk. She later suffered significant damage in a German air attack during the Battle of Crete.

Again in need of a major overhaul, *Warspite* arrived at the Puget Sound Naval Shipyard at Bremerton, Washington, for additional modifications and repairs that were completed in December shortly after the Japanese attack on Pearl Harbor. After lengthy service in the Indian Ocean, she joined Force H at Gibraltar and participated in the invasion of Sicily, Operation Husky where, in company with the battleships *Nelson, Rodney,* and *Valiant*, and the aircraft carriers *Illustrious* and *Formidable*, she took part in the Royal Navy bombardment of Sicily, laying heavy fire down on the German positions at Catania. In the punishing German air attacks of 8-9 September 1943, her gun crews shot down several enemy aircraft.

On 15 September, she operated in support of the Allied forces at Salerno. There she bombarded German positions with deadly accuracy, hitting her targets with nine of her twelve salvoes fired. The next day she was attacked by a squadron of German aircraft which caused great damage to the ship as well as killing nine sailors and wounding fourteen.

Her next journey involved being towed by U.S. Navy tugs to Malta. Her size and weight proved problematic for the tugs, however, and once during the long, slow trip all the tow lines broke and she began drifting sideways through the Straits of Messina. The little party finally reached Malta on 19 September and she underwent emergency repairs before being towed on to Gibraltar. She was then returned to Rosyth where her major repair work could be completed.

On 6 June 1944, *Warspite*, and several hundred other Allied vessels, lay off the shore of Normandy, a part of the Eastern Task Force of the D-Day invasion landings. Her heavy gun fire was concentrated on German defensive positions near Sword Beach. She then moved on to bombard in support of the British forces at Gold Beach. With her guns nearly worn out, she was ordered back to Rosyth to have them replaced and while steaming there she struck a magnetic mine. She went on through the Normandy campaign bombarding Brest, Le Havre, and Walcheren in support of an Allied amphibious assault in November.

The now very old and tired *Warspite* was approved for scrapping in July 1946 and on 19 April 1947,

HMS *Warspite*

she left Portsmouth and headed for the breaker's yard at Faslane on the River Clyde. Her continuing bad luck dogged her on this her final voyage. She ran into a severe storm and the hawser of one of her two tugs parted; the other tug then slipped its tow. In the heavy storm conditions, the commander dropped one of her two anchors in Mount's Bay, but it failed to hold and the force of the storm drove *Warspite* onto the mount. Her skeleton crew later managed to refloat her, only to see her run aground again in Prussia Cove. Her little crew was rescued by the Penlee lifeboat, but the badly damaged old battleship could not be refloated again, and a partial scrapping operation took place in that location.

In 1950, another attempt to refloat *Warspite* attracted the interest and attention of the BBC, the press, and a large crowd of spectators. But there was insufficient water to float her clear of the reef. In August the hulk was beached off St Michael's Mount and a further try to refloat her took place. Other mishaps befell the two Falmouth tugs engaged in the attempt, but with a supreme effort what was left of *Warspite* was moved 130 feet closer to shore. By the summer of 1955, all that was left of her had disappeared from view.

The Tirpitz

The German battleship *Tirpitz* was the second of the *Bismarck* class battleships constructed for the German Kriegsmarine during the Second World War. Commissioned in February 1941, she was named after Grand Admiral Alfred von Tirpitz who had been appointed Secretary of State in the German Navy Office where he immediately began the planning and formation of the new Imperial Navy's High Seas Fleet. He believed that the British Royal Navy would always be larger and in many ways superior to the German fleet, but that the British would of necessity have to spread that great fleet around the world. Therefore, he thought that the new German battle fleet needed only to be large enough to cope with that part of the British fleet that covered the North Sea and the English Channel. With an estimate of the size of the British Channel fleet and British warship building capacity, he determined that the German Navy would require the construction of sixty capital ships over the next twenty years. The German assembly actually authorized construction of thirty-eight battleships, twenty large cruisers and thirty-eight smaller cruisers. Early in the First World War, the commanders of the German Navy realized that the *Tirpitz* theory had been wrong; his assessment of the needs of the German Navy relative to the actual strength and capability of the British fleet was quite insufficient and the gap was widening. That gamble on the part of Tirpitz ended up costing him his influence with the Kaiser and isolation from naval circles. In March 1916, he resigned.

Like her sister ship *Bismarck*, *Tirpitz* had a main battery of eight fifteen-inch guns mounted in four twin turrets. She had a displacement of 42,900 tons and, after a series of wartime modifications, was 2,000 tons heavier than *Bismarck*. *Tirpitz* was 792 feet eight-inches long, with a beam of 118 feet and a draught of thirty feet six inches. She was capable of a thirty-five mph speed and had a range of 10,210 miles at twenty-two mph. Her complement included 103 officers and 1,962 men. In addition to her

The German battleship *Tirpitz*, seen here under construction, and her sister ship the *Bismarck*, were the largest warships ever built for the German Navy.

main armament, she mounted twelve 5.9-inch guns, sixteen 4.1-inch guns, sixteen 1.5-inch guns and twelve .79-inch flak guns, as well as eight twenty-one-inch torpedo tubes. She also carried four Arado Ar 196 floatplanes and was fitted with one double-ended catapult.

Built at Kriegsmarinewerft Wilhelmshaven, she was launched on 1 April 1939 and during her construction the harbour at Wilhelmshaven was repeated attacked by RAF bombers. None of the bombs struck the *Tirpitz*, but the attacks did slow her construction. Powered by three Brown, Boveri & Cie geared steam turbines and twelve oil-fired Wagner superheated boilers, she developed a total shaft horsepower of 163,026.

Under the terms of the Anglo-German Naval Agreement of June 1935, Germany agreed to restrict her fleet to thirty-five percent of that of Great Britain, but the terms of the 1922 Washington Naval Arms Limitation Agreement and the First London Naval Conference Agreement were still in force. Thus, a capital ship size limitation of 35,000 tons was still in place when, in 1936, the Germans defied those agreements and laid down their first genuine battleships since the end of the First World War, the 41,700-ton displacement *Bismarck* and the 42,000-ton displacement *Tirpitz*.

After her extensive sea trials, *Tirpitz* was stationed at Kiel and while she was there, the Germans invaded the Soviet Union. The German Navy established a temporary Baltic Fleet to contain the Soviet Fleet should it try to break out of its base at Leningrad. *Tirpitz* became the flagship of the squadron which was comprised of the heavy cruiser *Admiral Scheer*, the light cruisers *Köln, Nürnberg, Leipzig,* and *Emden*, several destroyers, and two flotillas of minesweepers. The Baltic Fleet, under the command of Admiral Otto Ciliax, conducted patrols off the Aaland Islands until 26 September 1941 and then

Tirpitz in Norwegian waters.

disbanded with *Tirpitz* returning to her training mission from her Kiel base. The RAF continued in its attempts to destroy her but was unsuccessful in the effort.

Convinced that the British were about to invade Norway, Adolf Hitler stated: "…the fate of the war will be decided there." He ordered Admiral Erich Raeder, Commander-in-Chief of the German Navy, to redeploy his fleet there. *Tirpitz* went to Trondheim where she would be well positioned to strike at the Russian convoys.

The British were intimidated by the mere presence of *Tirpitz* in Norwegian waters. It caused them to devote a large force of warships in protective duties for the North Atlantic convoys to Russia. They were determined to prevent the *Tirpitz* from breaking out into the Atlantic and menacing the Allied convoy vessels. Winston Churchill had said of her: "She rivetted our attention", even though for more than two years she had not sunk an enemy vessel or even fired on one.

Her time in the Norwegian fjords varied between arduous and monotonous for the crew. Frequent fuel shortages curtailed training, requiring her to remain sheltered much of the time under protective camouflage netting. The crew was mainly involved in maintaining the ship and manning her anti-aircraft defences. *Tirpitz*'s freedom of operation was further eroded with the withdrawal of her destroyer forces to go support Operation Cerberus, the English Channel dash of the battleships *Scharnhorst* and *Gneisenau*, together with the heavy cruiser *Prinz Eugen*. *Prinz Eugen* was torpedoed by a British submarine near the Faettenfjord and was left there disabled.

In March 1942, *Tirpitz* and *Admiral Scheer*, together with the destroyers *Z14*, *Z5*, *Z7*, *Z25*, and two torpedo boats, were all assigned to attack a homebound convoy QP-8 and the outbound convoy PQ-12 in special operation known as Sportpalast. But *Admiral Scheer*, with a top speed of thirty mph, wasn't fast enough to operate with *Tirpitz* and was left behind in port, along with the destroyer *Z5* and the two torpedo boats.

A Luftwaffe reconnaissance plane sighted convoy PQ-12 on 5 March near Jan Mayen Island, but inexplicably missed the presence of the battleship HMS *Duke of York*, the battlecruiser HMS *Renown*, and four destroyers, all escorting the convoy. Also unknown to the Germans was the distant British convoy cover being provided by the battleship HMS *King George V*, the aircraft carrier HMS *Victorious*, the heavy cruiser HMS *Berwick*, and six destroyers. The British, however, had been warned via Enigma code machine intercepts of the impending attack by *Tirpitz*, enabling them to quickly reroute the convoys. The British pursued *Tirpitz*, whose captain, Otto Ciliax, had decided to return the ship to port on 9 March, and that same day an air strike by twelve Fairey Albacore torpedo bombers was launched from *Victorious* to attack *Tirpitz* in three groups, but the German battleship evaded all of the attacks. Anti-aircraft gunners aboard *Tirpitz* shot down two of the torpedo bombers.

In the evening of the 13th, *Tirpitz* safely arrived in Trondheim, where she was again attacked on 30 March by thirty-three RAF Halifax bombers which scored no hits on the battleship but suffered the loss of five of their aircraft to anti-aircraft fire. In the night 27-28 April, another RAF bombing raid comprised of thirty-one Halifaxes and twelve Lancasters was also unsuccessful and also resulted in the loss of five aircraft. The RAF came back for another try the next evening, this time bringing twenty-three Halifaxes and eleven Lancasters, again for no results and this time the loss of two of the bombers.

A serious fuel shortage continued to plague the Germans and it took them fully three months to replenish the amount of fuel expended in the March effort to intercept the two Allied convoys. *Tirpitz* and the remainder of the German fleet in Norway would next go after convoy PQ-17 which had left Iceland on 27 June bound for Russia. PQ-17 was under the escort of the battleships HMS *Duke of York*, and the USS *Washington*, as well as the carrier *Victorious*. For the Germans, the attacking force of *Tirpitz*, *Admiral Hipper*, and six destroyers sailed out from Trondheim, and a second force consisting of the pocket battleships *Lutzow* and *Admiral Scheer*, together with six destroyers departed their ports at Narvik and Bogenfjord. That force lost the services of *Lutzow* and three of its destroyers on the way to rendezvous with the other force, when they struck uncharted rocks and had to return to port. Two torpedoes were fired at *Tirpitz* on her way to the rendezvous point, allegedly by a Soviet submarine, but both missiles missed their target. All of these German departures were being reported to the British Admiralty by Swedish intelligence sources, at which point the Admiralty ordered the convoy to disperse. Now the two German warship forces realized they had been detected and they aborted the operation, turning it over to the Luftwaffe and to U-boats in the area. The dye was cast against the British this time. The scattered vessels of PQ-17 were no longer able to be protected by their escorts. The German warships proceeded to attack and sink twenty-one of the thirty-four ships of the convoy. *Tirpitz* returned safely to Altafjord.

Tirpitz now needed a major overhaul and, because Hitler had forbidden the big ship to make the dangerous return voyage to Germany to have the work done, she was ordered to Trondheim for the repairs and maintenance. There, her local defences were improved, additional anti-aircraft guns were installed, and doubled anti-torpedo nets were erected around her. Because *Tirpitz* still provided a powerful threat to the Allies, it was decided to perform the overhaul work in various limited phases, so the ship would, for the most part, remain at least partially operational throughout the overhaul and could put to sea at any point should that be deemed essential.

The overhaul work was completed and *Tirpitz* began sea trials on 28 December, with gunnery trials conducted on 4 January.

The battleship *Scharnhorst* was transferred to Norway so that the two battleships might work together, this at a point when the Allied convoys to Russia had been temporarily halted. Now Admiral Raeder had been replaced by Hitler and the replacement was the U-bootwaffe's Admiral Karl Dönitz who ordered an attack on the island of Spitzbergen, where the British maintained a weather station and a refueling base. The base and settlements there were being defended by a garrison of 152 men from the Norwegian Armed Forces in exile. Under escort from ten destroyers, *Tirpitz* left port for Spitzbergen in a sneak approach. During the bombardment, she fired fifty-two main-battery shells and eighty-two rounds from her secondary weapons, in the first and only occasion in which she fired her main battery at an enemy target. An assault force then landed ashore, capturing seventy-four prisoners.

Now the British were utterly determined to do whatever was necessary to neutralize the threat posed by *Tirpitz* in the Arctic. At first they resorted to mini-attacks by X-Craft midget submarines, attacks aimed at the *Scharnhorst, Tirpitz*, and *Lutzow*. Towed into a nearby position by larger submarines, eight of the assigned ten X-Craft boats reached the target area and where they were to slip under the anti-torpedo nets to attach powerful mines to the hull bottoms of the target ships. Two of the craft managed to breach the defences of *Tirpitz* and plant their mines. The mines exploded, causing heavy damage to the battleship, one damaging turret Caesar, the second exploding near the port bow. One fuel tank was ruptured, armour plating was torn, and the double bottom was buckled. 1,400 tons of water quickly flooded the fuel tanks and the void spaces in the double bottom on the port side, causing a slight list which was soon balanced by counter-flooding on the starboard side. The severe flooding damaged all the turbo-generators in Generator Room 2, and all but one generator in Generator Room 1 were disabled by severed power cables or broken steam lines. Turret Dora was thrown from its bearings and could no longer be rotated; an especially problematic aspect for the Germans as there was no heavy-lift crane in Norway powerful enough to lift and reposition the turret back onto its bearings. Both of the ship's Arado Ar 196 floatplanes were destroyed in the explosions. The repair work on *Tirpitz* would last until 2 April 1944.

British intelligence knew that the repair work on *Tirpitz* was nearing completion in March, and prepared for an air strike against the battleship—Operation Tungsten—set for 4 April, but later rescheduled for the 3rd when Enigma decrypts revealed that *Tirpitz* was actually to depart early that morning for her sea trials. The British raid was to involve the fleet carriers *Furious* and *Victorious*, and the escort carriers *Emperor, Fencer, Pursuer*, and *Searcher*. It would send forty Barracuda dive-bombers carrying 1,600-pound armour-piercing bombs, escorted by forty fighters in two waves. The Barracudas scored fifteen direct hits and only two misses. The first wave of aircraft arrived at the target area at 5:29 a.m., just as the tugs were assisting *Tirpitz* from her mooring, with the second wave approaching at 6:30. Only two of the bombers were lost to German anti-aircraft gunners in the attack. In the attack, 122 of the ship's crew were killed and 316 wounded. Two of the 15cm turrets were destroyed, as were both of the Arado Ar 196 floatplanes. Serious fires broke out around the ship, and concussive shock from the bomb blasts disabled the starboard turbine engine. Saltwater used in fighting the fires reached the boilers, contaminating the feed water. More than 2,000 tons of seawater flooded the ship, most of it coming in through two holes in the side shell made by shell splinters from near misses. The water used to fight the fires also added to the flooding problem.

As the damage reports reached Admiral Dönitz, he ordered *Tirpitz* repaired regardless of cost even though he realized that she would no longer be fit for use in a surface action due to insufficient fighter support. The main repair work was completed by 2 June and the ship was able to travel under her own power again.

In Britain, a new series of carrier air strikes were planned for the coming three month period, but foul weather would result in their cancellation. In late August the bad weather finally broke and the Operations Goodwood were launched from the carriers *Furious, Formidable,* and *Indefatigable,* as well as the escort carriers *Nabob* and *Trumpeter,* all of them launching a total of thirty-eight bombers and forty-three escort fighters. Results of the attack were inconsequential.

With the bulk of the British Fleet Air Arm attacks having been largely ineffective, by mid-1944 the job of destroying *Tirpitz* was turned over to the Royal Air Force, specifically to No 5 Group, whose Lancaster heavy bombers brought six-ton Tallboy bombs to the task of penetrating the battleship's heavy armour. On Sunday, 15 September 1944, twenty-three Lancasters took off from a forward air base at Yagodnik in Russia, most of them armed with one Tallboy bomb. A single Tallboy hit on the bow of *Tirpitz* penetrated and exited the keel, exploding on the seabottom, causing severe flooding at the bow and a serious trim problem there. *Tirpitz* was now unseaworthy and limited to about twelve mph. Severe damage through concussive shock had wrecked the ship's fire control equipment. This time, German Naval Command decided to repair the battleship for use only as a floating gun platform. Quick patch-up repairs enabled her to to be moved 230 miles south to Tromso on 15 October.

Outside of Tromso lies the island of Hakoya, and it was there that *Tirpitz* lay moored on 29 October when thirty-two Lancasters of Nos 9 and 617 Squadrons attacked her again. While the bombing results were rather poor owing in part to bad weather over the target, one near miss caused an underwater explosion, damaging the port rudder and shaft of *Tirpitz,* as well as some flooding. After this attack the Germans built a substantial sandbank beneath and around the battleship in an effort to prevent her from capsizing in any additional attacks. They also installed new anti-torpedo nets around her. In her new role as a floating artillery platform, her fuel load was limited to just what was necessary to power the turbo-generators.

In early November 1944, planning began in London for Operation Catechism, the final British attack on *Tirpitz.* On the morning of 12 November, a force of thirty-two Lancasters from Nos 9 and 617 Squadrons dropped twenty-nine Tallboy bombs, scoring two direct hits and one near miss on *Tirpitz.* Other misses destroyed much of the specially-built sandbank the Germans had put in place to prevent the battleship from capsizing in such an attack. One of the bomb hits penetrated the main deck between turrets Anton and Bruno, but did not explode. Severe damage, however, resulted from a second hit amidships between the aircraft catapult and funnel. A large hole was made in the ship's side and bottom, destroying an entire section of belt armour and it is believed that a third bomb may have hit on the port side of turret Caesar. Substantial flooding resulted in a list to port of up to twenty degrees, increasing over the next ten minutes to forty degrees. The flooding progressed until, by 9:50, the list had climbed to sixty degrees and then seemed to stabilize. But eight minutes later, a huge explosion tore the roof off of turret Caesar. The roof and part of the rotating structure flew more than eighty feet into the air and passed over a group of *Tirpitz* crewmen swimming to shore. The great battleship then rolled over taking her superstructure into the sea bottom.

Bismarck

Bismarck was the lead ship of her class, her only sister ship being *Tirpitz*. She was built by Blohm und Voss, Hamburg, and was launched on 14 February 1939. Named after Chancellor Otto von Bismarck, she and the *Tirpitz* were the largest battleships ever built by Germany. Displacing 41,700 tons, she was 793 feet long, with a beam of 118 feet and a draught of thirty-one feet. In her trials she proved capable of nearly thirty-five mph. She had a range of 10,210 miles at twenty-two mph. Her armament included eight fifteen-inch main guns, twelve 5.9-inch guns, sixteen 4.1-inch guns, twelve .79-inch guns. She carried four Arado Ar 196 floatplanes which were launched on a double-ended catapult. Her ship's complement was 103 officers and 1,962 men.

The big ship left Hamburg on 15 September 1940 for her sea trials which would begin in Kiel Bay. From there she proceeded to Arcona on 28 September and on to Gotenhafen to continue her trials in the Gulf of Danzig. Completing the measured mile high-speed runs. While running an exercise to steer the ship only through altering propeller revolutions, it was found that *Bismarck* could only be kept on course that way with considerable difficulty. Even when running the outboard screws at full power, only a slight turning ability was available. She was brought back to her builders in December for slight adjustments and alterations through completion of the fitting out process. During her gunnery trials, when the main guns were fired for the first time, it was established that she was stable gun platform.

As the work was being completed on the new German battleship, she was visited by the Swedish naval attaché in Berlin, who returned to Sweden with his own detailed description of *Bismarck*. Soon, that descriptive information found its way to the Royal Navy via pro-British elements in the Swedish Navy. It gave the British their first credible description of the giant new warship, though it lacked much of the kind of information they craved, including displacement, radius of action, and top speed.

By early March 1941, *Bismarck* was taken to Kiel where she was stocked with all her ammunition, fuel, food and various supplies. While there the crew applied a coat of dazzle paint camouflage. On 12 March, an unsuccessful attempt was made by RAF bombers to attack the harbour area, without any effect on the battleship. Five days later she was escorted by an old icebreaker vessel to Gotenhafen for continuation of combat training.

Admiral Erich Raeder, at the head of OKM, the Naval High Command was intent on pursuing to use of his heaviest warships in the role of surface raiders against the Allied merchant convoys in the Atlantic. At that time, the *Scharnhorst* and *Gneisenau* battleships were back in their port at Brest in northern France, having just run such an Atlantic raid mission. Another candidate, the building battleship *Tirpitz*, sister ship to *Bismarck*, was nearing completion, and OKM decided to mount an operation involving all four of the battleships, with *Bismarck* and *Tirpitz* to rendezvous with the two Scharnhorst class vessels out in the Atlantic around 25 April. The finishing work on *Tirpitz* was delayed, however, and her commissioning delayed until 25 February, thus she was not ready for combat until the end of 1941. Additional problems plagued the mission of the four battleships when *Gneisenau* was attacked by the British with bombs and torpedoes while in drydock at Brest damaging her significantly, and *Scharnhorst*, meanwhile, developed boiler trouble making her unavailable for a long period.

Two other ships, the heavy cruisers *Admiral Hipper* and *Admiral Scheer*, scheduled to accompany the

left: The German battleship *Bismarck* was built at Blohm und Voss in Hamburg and launched on 14 February 1939; below: German Chancellor Adolf Hitler during his only visit to the *Bismarck*.

battleships on the mission, were laid up for repairs in Kiel when another attack by British bombers on supply depots in the port there added to the delay, as they would not be available for sea until late summer. The German admiral Günther Lütjens had been selected to command the mission and, in the circumstances, with the various problems and delays, wanted to reschedule the operation at least until either the *Scharnhorst* or *Tirpitz* became available to participate. But Naval High Command was impatient and chose to proceed instead with just the small force of *Bismarck* and the heavy cruiser *Prinz Eugen*.

Adolf Hitler in company with Generalfeldmarschal Wilhelm Keitel visited *Bismarck* and *Tirpitz* on 5 May 1941 and were treated to an extensive tour of the two battleships. After the tour, there was a conversation between Hitler and Admiral Lütjens about the planned Atlantic operation. Less than two weeks later, the admiral announced that *Bismarck* and *Prinz Eugen* were ready for the operation and he was proceeding with it on the evening of 19 May. In preparation and support of it, an assemblage of eighteen supply ships were to be positioned along the convoy routes between Halifax, Nova Scotia, and Britain and four U-boats would be used along the routes to scout for the big raiders.

When the operation began, the crew of *Bismarck* had grown to 2,221 officers and men, some of whom had been added to crew any captured vessels in the mission. The Battleship left Gotenhafen at two in morning of 19 May and headed for the Straits of Denmark where she was joined by *Prinz Eugen* at 11:25 a.m. which had come from Cape Arkona the evening before. In their escort were three destroyers, *Z10, Z16,* and *Z23,* as well as a flotilla of minesweepers, and the Luftwaffe provided air cover for the first portion of the journey. The skipper of *Bismarck*, Kapitän zur See Ernst Lindemann, told the crew about their mission at noon on the 20th. As he was doing so, a flight of Swedish reconnaissance aircraft happened to sight the German warships and reported the sighting. Early in the af-

Pride of the German Navy, the *Bismarck* in profile.

ternoon, the Germans ships were shadowed for a few hours by a Swedish cruiser which reported seeing: "Two large warships, three destroyers, five escort vessels, and about ten aircraft passing Marstrand, course 205°/20'." Both Lütjens and Lindemann now knew that their surprise factor was lost. The Swedish naval report quickly arrived at the Admiralty in London and the code-breakers at Bletchley Park decrypted messages confirming that an Atlantic raid was imminent. Two reconnaissance Spitfires were then sent out to patrol the Norwegian coast in search of the German flotilla. Meanwhile, German air reconnaissance was able to confirm that three battleships, an aircraft carrier, and four cruisers were still at anchor in Scapa Flow, causing Lütjens to believe that, to that point at least, the British were still in the dark about his mission. The German flotilla arrived at the Norwegian coast late in the evening 20 May, detaching the minesweepers there, while the two raiders and their escorts proceeded their northern journey. The next day, German radio officers aboard *Prinz Eugen* intercepted a British signal ordering recce aircraft in the area to search for the two raiders. A day later the German flotilla anchored at Grimstadfjord near Bergen, where they were seen and photographed by an RAF Spitfire flying at 26,000 feet over *Bismarck*.

With that information at hand, the British Admiralty ordered the new battleship *Prince of Wales*, the battlecruiser *Hood*, and six destroyers to join with the two Royal Navy cruisers then patrolling the Denmark Strait, while putting the balance of the Home Fleet in Scapa on high alert status. The RAF immediately sent a force of eighteen bombers to attack the enemy warships, but worsening weather conditions prevented them finding their target.

The small German naval force of *Bismarck*, *Prinz Eugen*, and three escorting destroyers departed Bergen at 7:30 p.m. of 21 May for the Arctic Ocean. It was midnight when Admiral Raeder finally informed Hitler of the raiding operation. Hitler approved it with little enthusiasm. At noon on 22 May,

Lütjens directed his two big warships towards the Denmark Strait and the open Atlantic. There in the very early hours of 23 May, he ordered the two ships to make thirty-one mph in the dash through the Strait. As the pair steamed through, *Prinz Eugen* trailed *Bismarck* by about 800 yards in very misty, greatly reduced visibility of little more than 4,000 yards. By 10:00 a.m., the two ships were running into some ice and had to reduce speed to twenty-eight mph. By mid-day they were north of Iceland, having to resort to zig-zagging to avoid ice floes. That evening at about 7:20, radar operators in the German vessels had detected the presence of the cruiser HMS *Suffolk* at a distance of about 14,000 yards. Decrypting signals from *Suffolk*, the German radio interceptors confirmed that the German warships' location had indeed been reported to London.

At this point, Lütjens permitted the crew of *Prinz Eugen* to engage the *Suffolk*, but in the heavy mist the captain of *Prinz Eugen* could not clearly see his target and held his fire. While he did so, *Suffolk* pulled back to a safer distance from which it shadowed the German ships. At 8:30 p.m., the heavy cruiser *Norfolk* joined *Suffolk*, but as it did so, it approached too close to the German warships. *Bismarck* fired five salvoes, of which, three straddled *Norfolk*, dropping a shower of shell splinters on her decks. Putting out a smoke screen, the *Norfolk* hurried into the relative safety of a fog bank. *Bismarck*'s firing negatively affected her radar, which caused Lütjens to order *Prinz Eugen* to take station ahead of *Bismarck* and use the lead ship's radar capability to scout for the small formation.

A strange cat-and-mouse game began around ten that evening when Lütjens had *Bismarck* steam through a 180° turn in an attempt at surprising the two British heavy cruisers chasing him. The German battleship was virtually invisible in the heavy murk, but the radar of *Suffolk* detected the ruse, enabling *Suffolk* to escape. The British cruisers continued their shadowing of the German force all night, sending location reports back to the Admiralty. The weather the next morning was fair, the sky clear, and at just after 5:00 a.m., the hydrophone operators aboard *Prinz Eugen* detected two unidentified ships approaching the German formation at a range of twenty-three miles.

Shortly before six that morning, German lookouts saw smoke on the horizon from what were soon identified as the *Hood* and the *Prince of Wales*, and Vizeadmiral Lütjens ordered the crews of his ships to battle stations. Then the main guns of Hood opened fire, followed almost immediately by those of *Prince of Wales*. *Hood*'s gun crews were shooting at *Prinz Eugen*, mistaking it initially for *Bismarck*. *Prince of Wales* was firing on *Bismarck*. After a few moments hesitation, Lütjens finally granted Lindemann permission to return fire from *Bismarck*.

The approaching positions of the ships of both sides were such that only the two German warships were able to shoot full broadsides, and both were firing on *Hood*. Soon after opening fire, *Prinz Eugen* put an eight-inch high-explosive shell into one of *Hood*'s magazines which started a large, but containable fire. With the range fixed, the guns of *Bismarck* began sending accurate salvoes at *Hood*, as well as concentrating secondary fire on *Prince of Wales*. At this point both *Hood* and *Prince of Wales* were sailing a parallel course to that of the Germans. Lütjens wanted to keep both British warships under constant fire and ordered *Prinz Eugen* to change the focus of her fire onto *Prince of Wales*.

By 6:00 a.m. *Hood* was turning when she was struck by a salvo from *Bismarck*. Of the lot, two shells were short and hit the water nearby. But one of the big, armour-piercing shells penetrated the thin deck armour of *Hood*, into her rear ammunition magazine and exploded more than 100 tons of cordite propellent. The enormous blast broke *Hood*'s back between the rear funnel and the main mast. While the forward part of the ship continued briefly under momentum, very quickly the sea water rushed in flooding it and sending it high into the air. At the same time, the stern rose up and,

below: One of the last photos of *Bismarck* before her demise; bottom: A still from the 1960 film *Sink The Bismarck!*

within eight minutes of opening fire on *Hood*, the Germans had sent her to the bottom with all but three of her 1,419 crewmen.

Now it was the turn of *Prince of Wales* to receive the full attention of *Bismarck*. In her very first salvo, the German battleship put a shell into the bridge of *Prince of Wales*. The shell failed to explode, but in passing through the command centre, killed all present except Captain John Leach, the ship's commander, and one other man. Both of the German warships maintained their fire on *Prince of Wales* and inflicted severe damage to her. The new British battleship, which was still carrying some civilian ship-building technicians, managed three hits on *Bismarck*: one in the forecastle above the waterline, but sufficiently holing the hull to enable some flooding; a second shell hitting just below the armoured belt and exploding on contact with the torpedo bulkhead for minimal damage; and a third shell that went through one of the boats aboard the Prince before destroying the floatplane catapult.

With only two of his main guns still operative, Captain Leach ordered the *Prince of Wales* to retreat, which she executed in a wide turn while laying a smoke screen to cover her withdrawal. Lindemann wanted to chase the British battleship, but Lütjens rejected that, citing his operational orders. Instead, the formation commander ordered *Bismarck* and *Prinz Eugen* to head for the North Atlantic. In the action, the shell hit in *Bismarck*'s bow caused flooding which contaminated fuel oil stored there. Lütjens, insistent upon operating at high speed, adamantly refused to slow the battleship enough for damage control teams to repair the large shell hole which, as they raced north, became larger, increasing the flooding. The flooding was causing 9° list and a 3° trim by the bow.

Around eight that morning, Lütjens made his battle report to OKM, and stated his intention to detach *Prinz Eugen* for commerce raiding and take *Bismarck* to St Nazaire for repairs. Later he ordered *Prinz Eugen* to fall back and inspect to determine the severity of the oil leakage from *Bismarck*'s bow. *Prinz Eugen* confirmed broad streams of oil in both sides of *Bismarck*'s wake. Soon, another observer, a British Sunderland flying boat, reported the oil slick from *Bismarck* to *Suffolk* and *Norfolk*, which were now in company with the damaged *Prince of Wales*.

The loss of *Hood* spurred Prime Minister Churchill and the Admiralty to find and sink *Bismarck*. The Admiralty ordered all British warships in the area to join the hunt for *Bismarck* and *Prinz Eugen*. It also directed the light cruisers *Arethusa*, *Birmingham*, and *Manchester* to patrol Denmark Strait in case *Bismarck* might elect to retrace her route. Two elderly *Revenge* class battleships, *Revenge* and *Ramillies*, were also ordered into the hunt, which now numbered six battleships and battlecruisers, two aircraft carriers, thirteen cruisers, and twenty-one destroyers. By the end of the afternoon, the crew of *Prince of Wales* had restored nine of her ten main guns to operation, allowing her to take the lead of the formation chasing the *Bismarck*.

In the late afternoon, the weather in the area got worse. Lütjens was unable to successfully detach *Prinz Eugen* and cover her withdrawal from the eyes of the British cruisers' crews which, in any event, were tracking both German ships on radar. At 6:14 p.m., he succeeded in detaching *Prinz Eugen* and then turned *Bismarck* to face *Suffolk*, which then retreated rapidly. Both *Prince of Wales* and *Bismarck* fired a series of main gun salvoes at each other without effect. Bismarck returned to her previous course with three British warships taking up station to her port side. Though damaged in the day's main engagement, *Bismarck* was still capable of at least thirty-one mph, and the British knew that unless she could be slowed somehow, they would be unable to prevent her reaching St Nazaire.

In the afternoon of 25 May, the British aircraft carrier *Victorious*, together with four light cruisers, were detached and sent off to position themselves for the carrier to launch her torpedo bombers.

Six Fairey Fulmar fighters and nine Fairey Swordfish torpedo bombers were launched from *Victorious* at ten that evening. Inexperience among the air crews nearly resulted in their erroneously attacking the *Norfolk* instead of the *Bismarck*, and *Bismarck*'s anti-aircraft gun crews were alerted to the incoming raid. As the planes approached the German battleship, her gun crews depressed her main and secondary guns to create huge splashes in the path of the low-flying attackers. The battleship managed to evade eight of the nine torpedoes launched at her, but the ninth struck amidships causing only minor damage. The high-speed maneuvring of the battleship to evade the torpedoes increased the flooding in the forward shell hole, leading eventually to the abandonment of the port side number two boiler room. Now the crew was forced to reduce speed due to the loss of two boilers on the port shaft, decreasing fuel levels from the leakage, and the increasing bow trim caused by the shell hit. Now *Bismarck* could make no more than eighteen mph. Following some temporary repairs by divers, she was able to resume a speed of twenty-three mph.

The chase moved into open waters and the British warships had to begin zig-zagging to avoid U-boats that might be present. Through a series of high-speed turns, Lütjens was able to successfully break radar contact with *Bismarck*'s British pursuers, and actually circled back behind them. At daylight the British force commander ordered his three ships to disperse and begin a visual search for the German battleship. Soon, that search became almost panic-driven, with most of the British ships running dangerously low on fuel.

A new factor, Force H, centred on the aircraft carrier *Ark Royal*, was rushing up from Gibraltar, but was still roughly a day away. Meanwhile, Lütjens in *Bismarck* didn't realise that he had actually escaped from the British warships and sent some lengthy radio messages to his Naval Group West in Paris, messages that were intercepted by the British. But mistakes in the British plotting of the bearings in his messages led to the British warships being misdirected in the chase, and by the time the errors had been caught, *Bismarck* had disappeared.

The British were actually well informed about the German plans for *Bismarck*. They were intercepting various German signals and decrypting them and knew, for example, that Lütjens had been ordered to take the battleship to Brest. They knew, too, that certain German Air Force units were being relocated to the area near Brest to provide support for the movements and sheltering of *Bismarck*—this from the French Resistance. The British were then able to focus units of the Royal Navy toward Brest and the waters through which the *Bismarck* would have to pass. The great British force being mustered in the pursuit of the German battleship now included a squadron of RAF Coastal Command Consolidated PBY Catalina flying boats based in Northern Ireland. It was one of these PBYs, an aircraft flown by U.S. Navy Ensign Leonard Smith, that found *Bismarck*, slightly less than 800 miles northwest of Brest, and less than a day from the massive German naval base there.

Only the *Ark Royal* and Force H, under the command of Admiral James Somerville, offered any real hope for the British catching and destroying *Bismarck* before the battleship reached the sanctuary of the base in France. Most of the Royal Navy warships in the region, including *Repulse, Prince of Wales, Suffolk,* and *Victorious* were seriously low on fuel by this point and had to break off their part in the search. Only *Rodney* and *George V*, of the bigger ships, remained in the hunt, but they were simply too far away. The Swordfish bombers of *Ark Royal* were out flying a search pattern in the mid-morning of 26 May when Ensign Smith in the Catalina found the German battleship. Around the same time, several of the Swordfish aircraft also located *Bismarck* at a point roughly seventy miles from *Ark Royal*. As soon as they returned to the carrier, Somerville ordered them armed with torpedoes and the cruiser *Sheffield* was detached to shadow the enemy battleship. The Swordfish pilots, however, had not been informed of *Sheffield*'s assignment, and one of the many accidents of war occurred when they mistook the *Sheffield* for the *Bismarck* and attacked her with their new magnetic-detonator torpedoes. Fortunately, the detonators failed to function and *Sheffield* escaped.

The Swordfish planes returned to *Ark Royal* and this time they were loaded with contact-detonator torpedoes. Fifteen of the planes were launched at 7:10 p.m. Three hours later they were in position and ready to start their attack, descending through the cloud cover. As they dropped towards *Bismarck*, the main gun crews of the German battleship began firing on *Sheffield* and were able to straddle her with their second salvo. Three of the cruiser's sailors were killed and several wounded by the shell fragments that showered her. As Sheffield managed a hasty retreat under the cover of a smoke screen, the attack by the Swordfish began. Realizing she was under attack, *Bismarck* entered a series of turns, as violent as a ship of her size is capable of making, as her anti-aircraft guns reacted against the incoming torpedo bombers. All but two of the torpedoes missed their mark, but one struck amidships on the port side, under the main armour belt. When it exploded, the damage was limited by *Bismarck*'s underwater protection system and the belt armour. There was some structural damage and relatively minor flooding. It was the second torpedo that did the damage when it smashed into the stern of the battleship on the port side adjacent the port rudder shaft. It's explosion seriously damaged the coupling on the port rudder assembly, preventing the rudder from engaging, and locking it in a 12° turn to port. There was also substantial shock damage from the explosion. The crew struggled in several attempts to regain the steering control of the great ship, and did manage to effect repairs on the starboard rudder, but could do nothing for the jammed port rudder. Lütjens rejected a suggestion of one crew member that explosives be used to try and sever the damaged port rudder. He worried that an ancillary effect of the blasting might damage the screws, leaving *Bismarck* entirely helpless. At 9:15 p.m. he had to report that the battleship was unmanoeuvrable.

The movement of the giant battleship was now limited to steaming in a big circle. She had no escape from the approaching British warships. The battleships *Rodney* and *King George V* were in the area, as were the heavy cruisers *Dorsetshire* and *Norfolk*. In a memorable signal to headquarters, Lütjens said: "Ship unmanoeuvrable. We will fight to the last shell. Long live the Führer." The German naval headquarters replied with messages meant to build up morale, but deep depression was flooding the crew as the reality of their situation sank in. *Bismarck*'s gun crews slowly desisted their attack on *Sheffield* and the British warship left the area in the low visibility murk of the evening. The five waiting British destroyers present now had the assignment of staying in contact with the German battleship through the rest of the night.

At just before eleven that night, *Bismarck* turned on the enemy destroyers and opened fire with her main batteries. The destroyers harrassed the German battleship throughout the night and into the following morning. They illuminated her in the darkness with starshells and sent several torpedoes her way, but none of them were hits. In a desperate act, the crew attempted to launch one of the ship's Arado Ar 196 floatplanes to take the *Bismarck*'s war diary, film footage of her battle action with the *Hood,* and other documents to safety. For an hour in the early morning they struggled with the launch procedure, but damage to the plane's catapult by one of the shells from *Prince of Wales* had left the catapult unuseable and unrepairable. Finally, they were ordered to simply shove the plane overboard.

With daylight on the morning of the 27th, the British battleships *Rodney* and *King George V* steamed directly at *Bismarck*. It was their intention to reach a point about nine miles from the German war ship, where they would turn south to parallel it before opening fire. A lookout aboard *King George V* sighted *Bismarck* at 8:43 a.m. at a distance of 25,000 yards, Within four minutes the main guns of both British battleships opened fire. The Germans quickly returned fire and straddled *Rodney* with their second salvo. The ships of both sides closed and soon began firing their secondary guns too. A major blow to *Bismarck* came at 9:02 when a sixteen-inch shell from *Rodney* blasted her superstructure, killing hundreds of men and heavily damaging the two forward turrets. Reports from survivors indicated that this blast killed both Lindemann and Lütjens along with the entire bridge staff. It also disabled the forward main battery. Another casualty of the shell was the main gunnery control station. By 9:30, all of *Bismarck's* main battery turrets had been made inoperative.

Bismarck was an utter ruin by 10:00, and was burning from one end to the other. She was low in the water by the stern and lay at a 20° list to port. Now *Rodney* moved in to a distance of just 3,000 yards and continued firing into the badly crippled battleship. The British would cease fire if the crew of *Bismarck* would lower their ensigns or show signs of abandoning ship. In what is probably the only such incident in history of a battleship torpedoing another battleship, *Rodney* sent two torpedoes towards *Bismarck*, claiming one hit. Then came the moment when *Bismarck's* First Officer gave the command to abandon ship and told the engine room crews to set scuttling charges and open the watertight doors. As many of the engineering crewmen were climbing towards the main deck to leave the battleship, they could hear the demolition charges detonating. When many of the men reached the main deck, another huge blast killed about 100 of them.

By 10:30 the British warships had fired more than 2,800 shells at *Bismarck* and achieved more than 400 hits. The German battleship was still afloat and, with all of the British vessels running low on fuel, the *Dorsetshire* was ordered to sink the *Bismarck* with torpedoes. Her crew launched two torpedoes, hitting with one on the starboard side of the German ship. *Dorsetshire* then steamed around to put another torpedo into *Bismarck* on the port side. Now *Bismarck* was listing to the point that her deck was partially awash. Then, at 10:35, she capsized to port and began sinking by the stern. At 10:40 she was gone.

Roughly 400 German sailors were in the water awaiting rescue as *Dorsetshire* and the destroyer *Maori* approached with ropes lowered. The rescue effort continued until 11:40 when lookouts in *Dorsetshire* sighted what they believed to be a U-boat. The two British ships had picked up 110 survivors between them when they had to call off the rescue work and depart. A few more German crewmen were saved by a U-boat and a German trawler. Of the *Bismarck's* crew of more than 2,200 men, 114 survived.

Yamato

The heaviest, most powerfully armed, and possibly the most capable battleship ever built, the *Yamato* was the pride of the Imperial Japanese Navy from the time of her launching in August 1940. The lead ship of the *Yamato* class, she shared her characteristics with her sister ship, *Musashi*. Named for the ancient Japanese province of Yamato, she displaced 70,000 tons, was 840 feet long, with a beam of 127 feet and a draught of thirty-six feet. She was capable of a thirty-one mph top speed and had a range of 8,290 miles at a speed of eighteen mph. She was armed with nine eighteen-inch main guns, six 6.1-inch guns, twenty-four five-inch guns, 162 .98-inch anti-aircraft guns, and four .52-inch anti-aircraft guns. She carried seven small aircraft and mounted two catapult launchers for them.

The design and construction of *Yamato* resulted following Japan's withdrawal from the League of Nations in 1934 and from the limitations of the 1922 Washington Naval Treaty. The design and construction of the big battleship was carried out in utmost secrecy in an effort to hide it from the Americans. Japan was realistic about their limited ability to produce warships of the greatest capability, and in *Yamato* and *Musashi*, they hoped to have battleships that could, both literally and figuratively, outgun those of the United States. The nine main battery guns of *Yamato* were the largest calibre naval guns ever installed in a warship. Each gun was capable of firing a high-explosive or armour-piercing shell some twenty-six miles.

In February 1942, *Yamato* became the flagship of Admiral Isoroku Yamamoto and the Imperial Japanese Navy Combined Fleet. The admiral was planning to take on the warships of the U.S. Navy at Midway Island and lure the enemy vessels into a trap there. But things didn't work out according

to his plan. American code-breakers had cracked the Japanese naval code and knew about the Midway mission. In the action there, four of Japan's big fleet aircraft carriers were destroyed, as were 332 Japanese aircraft. The admiral had widely dispersed the main warships of his fleet as part of the plan to entrap the American ships. As such, the Japanese battleship group was too distant to take part in the battle.

During the great Guadalcanal Campaign in 1942, *Yamato* was anchored at Truk, unable to play her part in the action due to a shortage of appropriate ammunition for shore bombardment, and her unusually high fuel consumption. She acquired a nickname among the crews of Japan's cruisers and destroyers in the South Pacific—Hotel Yamato—as, in the entire battle for Guadalcanal, she left port in Truk only once, for a single day and did not depart until 8 May 1943.

On Christmas Day 1943, *Yamato* and her sister ship *Musashi* were ferrying troops and equipment from Yokosuka, Japan, to Truk, when her task group was discovered by the U.S. Navy submarine *Skate*. The sub crew launched four torpedoes at *Yamato*, one of which hit on her starboard side near the stern. An eighty-two-foot hole was ripped in the hull and the ship took on about 3,000 tons of water, leading to repairs in Kure which took nearly a month and were followed by modifications and refitting lasting into April 1944. In June, *Yamato* was part of a re-organized fleet under the command of Vice-Admiral Jisaburo Ozawa when they took part in the Battle of the Philippine Sea, which the Amer-

The Imperial Japanese Navy battleship *Ise* was partially sunk in shallow water during an air attack by bomb-carrying F4U Corsair fighters on 28 July 1945. She was berthed in the Kure Dockyard at the time.

ican airmen involved called 'The Great Marianas Turkey Shoot.' In that action, the Japanese lost three aircraft carriers and 426 aircraft. *Yamato* took no significant part in the battle.

After undergoing an extensive fire-proofing programme, *Yamato*, in company with the battleships *Musashi, Kongo,* and *Nagato,* together with eleven cruisers and destroyers, left for the Lingga Islands where they arrived on 16 July, remaining there for the next three months.

In late October, as part of the IJN's First Striking Force, *Yamato* was involved in one of history's greatest naval engagements, the Battle of Leyte Gulf. American troops were landing in an invasion on the island of Leyte in the Philippines. In the hazardous transit of the Palawan Passage, the Japanese warship force was attacked on 23 October by the American submarines *Dace* and *Darter* which sank two of the heavy cruisers, one of which had been flagship of the task force and its commander, Admiral Takeo Kurita, who then transferred his flag to *Yamato*. The next day was another bad one for the Japanese force, which suffered the loss of three additional heavy cruisers. Aircraft from the U.S. carrier *Essex* caused moderate damage to *Yamato* with armour-piercing bombs which led to the battleship taking on more than 2,000 tons of water. In the action that day, the great battleship *Musashi* was struck by seventeen torpedoes and nineteen bombs and was sunk.

On 24 October, the main U.S. defensive force under the command of Admiral William Halsey, Jr. left Leyte to pursue the Japanese Northern Force, which in fact, was a decoy force made up of the fleet aircraft carrier *Zuikaku*, three light carriers, and several more warships. This group succeeded in drawing the five American fleet carriers and five light carriers (with more than 600 aircraft aboard them), six battleships, eight cruisers, and more than forty destroyers away from the Leyte area. In the dark of that evening, Admiral Kurita's warships made their way through the San Bernardino Strait. The next morning, in the Battle off Samar, they attacked the American formation that had remained there to give close support to the invading U.S. troops. The small American group included six escort carriers, three destroyers and four destroyer escorts. This was the only occasion in which *Yamato* engaged enemy surface targets. In the action she scored several hits on the U.S. Navy ships including the escort carrier USS *Gambier Bay*. Popularly referred to as "Combustable Vulnerable Expendable", the CVE escort carriers suffered heavily in the action. *Gambier Bay* was hit by several high-explosive shells from the Japanese warship *Chikuma*, leaving her dead in the water. Fires were burning furiously in her and three Japanese cruisers closed in for the kill. At 9:07 a.m. the escort carrier capsized and sank— the first and only U.S. aircraft carrier sunk by naval gunfire in the Second World War. 800 of her crew survived and were rescued.

Another American escort carrier, the USS *St Lo*, while under gun attack by an enemy cruiser, experienced a kamikaze suicide attack at 10:47 when a Japanese aircraft crashed into the flight deck of the escort carrier. The explosion of the bomb the plane had been carrying was sufficient to sink the carrier, with the loss of 114 seamen.

The relatively light American surface ships, supported by Wildcat fighters and Avenger torpedo bombers then launched a savage assault on Kurita's ships. In the mistaken belief that he was engaging in battle with up to six American fleet aircraft carriers, three cruisers, two destroyers and a great many aircraft, Kurita ordered his task force to retreat. In the encounter, *Yamato* incurred minor damage, but in the retreat she experienced additional damage and twenty-one casualties killed or injured.

The last major assault in the American island-hopping Pacific campaign of the war prior to the invasion of the Japanese mainland, was the invasion of the island of Okinawa set for April 1945. To counter that effort, the Imperial Japanese Navy prepared Operation Ten-Go, committing the involvement of most of the nation's remaining naval surface strength. The mission called for the battleship *Yamato*, accompanied by the cruiser *Yahagi* and eight destroyers, to sail to Okinawa to operate there in concert with army and kamikaze units. *Yamato* was ordered to be beached there to become an unsinkable gun platform and fight there until destroyed. She was loaded to capacity with ammunition for the fight and was, supposedly, fueled for a one-way voyage. The Japanese warship force was designated the Surface Special Attack Force and departed Tokuyama in the afternoon of 6 April.

Operation Ten-Go was no secret to the Americans, who had intercepted and decoded the enemy transmissions containing details of the plan. Progress of the Surface Special Attack Force was confirmed through sightings of the force by U.S. Navy submarines as it was travelling through the Bungo Strait. The subs reported *Yamato*'s position to the main American carrier strike force. Initially, the American Admiral Raymond Spruance ordered the six U.S. battleships then engaged in the shore bombardment of Okinawa, to be prepared for surface action against *Yamato*. Spruance was overruled, however, by Admiral Marc Mitscher who favoured strikes by his carrier aircraft. As a contingency though, Mitscher sent the American battleships, seven cruisers and twenty-one destroyers to meet the Japanese naval force before it could threaten the U.S. transport ships and landing craft.

Shortly after eight in the morning of 7 April two U.S. Navy flying boats appeared and began shadowing *Yamato* and the Japanese force for the next five hours. At 11:00 several F6F Hellcat fighters arrived overhead to take on any enemy aircraft that might appear. At 12:30 a force of 280 bomber and torpedo bomber aircraft arrived and the vessels of the Surface Special Attack Force increased speed and began circling *Yamato* in a defensive move.

At 12:41 two bombs struck the battleship, destroying two of her anti-aircraft mounts and blowing a huge hole in the deck. Another bomb destroyed the radar room and a starboard aft gun mount. Two more bombs then virtually destroyed an aft centreline turret and its magazine, with only one man surviving from the turret crew.

Yamato was hit by a torpedo on her forward port side. As many as three further torpedoes struck the ship on the port side near the engine room and one of the boiler rooms. A lull in the attack occurred at 12:47. The battleship was now listing at about 5° to port, but counterflooding reduced the list to 1°. One of the boiler rooms was disabled, reducing *Yamato*'s speed slightly. In the attack thus far, several of the crews of her many 25mm anti-aircraft guns had been killed or incapacitated, greatly reducing her fighting ability.

A second Allied attack began around 1:00 p.m. High-flying dive-bombers appeared overhead just as dozens of torpedo bombers approached from various directions at just above sea level. The remaining anti-aircraft gun crews of the battleship were simply overwhelmed by the extraordinary number of targets. The Japanese crews, in their desperation to break up the coordinated Allied attack, began loading and firing Beehive shells that were fused to explode one second after being fired, or about 3,000 feet out from *Yamato*, but to little real effect. At that point, she was again struck by torpedoes; with three hits on the port side, one of them adding to previous torpedo damage in the hull and extending the flooding there. *Yamato* was soon listing up to 18° to port, forcing the crew to counterflood all the remaining starboard void spaces in order to reduce the list to about 10°. *Yamato* was still not in genuine danger of sinking, though the degree of list now meant that her main battery could not fire and her maximum speed capability was reduced to twenty-one mph. Again, there was a lull in the action.

At 1:40 p.m., the third enemy aircraft attack came, by far the most serious of the battle. Four bombs slammed into the superstructure of *Yamato* with heavy casualties to the crew. These blasts were followed shortly by four additional torpedo strikes, three of them exploding on the port side and adding substantially to the major flooding of the port inner engine room, another fire room, and the steering gear room. The auxiliary steering room was already underwater and now the battleship lost all ability to manoeuvre and was jammed in a starboard turn. It is believed, but cannot be confirmed, that the fourth torpedo of this spread probably hit the starboard outer engine room which, together with three other spaces on that side, was being counterflooded to reduce the port list. The water was pouring in at such a rate that many crewmen were trapped in the spaces and could not escape.

Yamato's captain gave the order to abandon ship at 2:02 p.m. The speed had dropped to just twelve mph and the dangerous list was increasing. Several major fires raged out of control around the ship and alarms were sounding on the bridge warning of critical temperatures in the forward main battery magazines. The crew would have flooded the magazines to prevent explosions, but the required pumping stations for that action had been disabled by earlier flooding.

A final flight of American torpedo bombers roared in and attacked *Yamato* on her starboard side and her list was so severe that the torpedoes struck the bottom of her hull and she continued her slow roll to port. At 2:20 p.m. all power in the battleship was lost. At 2:23 she capsized and her main gun turrets fell off. Many of her crew who were in the sea swimming away from the sinking *Yamato*, were drawn back towards the ship by the suction created as she rolled over. Then one of her two bow magazines detonated in a massive, violent explosion that raised a mushroom cloud nearly four miles above the sea, a cloud visible nearly 100 miles away on the home island of Kyushu. It is estimated that at least 2,055 members of her 2,332-man crew were lost in the sinking by eleven torpedoes and six bombs.

The heaviest armoured vessel ever built, *Yamato* was ultimately sacrificed in a one-way mission to the island of Okinawa. There, she was assigned to destroy the enemy invasion fleet or, failing that, she was to be run aground and use her huge firepower in support of the Japanese defenders. She was sunk by torpedo and bomb hits on 7 April 1945. It is estimated that only 280 of her 2,332-man crew survived.

Iowa Class

They are *Iowa* (BB-61), *New Jersey* (BB-62), *Missouri* (BB-63), and *Wisconsin* (BB-64), the fast battle-ships of the *Iowa* class . . . the last battleships in the world. The very last of the last is, in fact, *Missouri*, because, while the building of *Wisconsin* was started later than that of *Missouri*, and though *Wisconsin* had a higher hull number, *Missouri* was actually the last battleship to be completed, to serve, and survive.

Historically, battlecruisers have been faster in general than battleships, but they have also had lighter armour protection and as such were more vulnerable to enemy attack. The greatest navies in the world wanted a warship that combined the best characteristics of battlecruisers and battleships, in a package made up of great speed, massive firepower, and excellent armoured protection. The speed advantage held by the battlecruiser over the battleship dissolved as substantial improvements in gun calibre, fire control, and ballistic efficiency arrived.

By the early 1930s, the United States Navy was giving serious consideration to the development of an entirely new, fast battleship. As American interests in the Pacific region developed after the end of the First World War, the government began to relocate much of the U.S. warship fleet on the west coast to be in a better position to protect and defend those vital interests and American possessions. By the middle of the decade, American naval strategists were clear on the liklihood of Japan being America's next wartime adversary. The Japanese naval planners, meanwhile, were still bristling under the perception of having been forced into the role of secondary naval power by the prohibitive terms of the 1922 Washington Naval Arms Limitation Treaty. Under a veil of secrecy, they struck out on their own to become a major naval power despite the treaty, embarking on a new programme of war-ship reconstruction, modernization, and radical new design and construction, all aimed at emerging as the most formidable naval fighting force ever.

The USS *Iowa* (BB-61) was the lead ship of her class of four American fast battleships, the last great battleships to be built. All four of the *Iowa*s survived the Second World War and subsequent conflicts and all are now serving as naval museums. The *Missouri*, (BB-63) was selected to be the site of the surrender signing by Japanese and Allied representatives on 2 September 1945 while the ship was anchored in Tokyo Bay.

American military intelligence knew that the Japanese were developing a new class of super-battleship, one that would be an unacceptable threat to the United States, her navy, and her strategic interests. To counter that threat to some extent, the U.S. forged ahead with the development of her own advanced battleship design, the 37,000-ton *North Carolina* Class. Armed with nine sixteen-inch main guns in three turrets, she would have a top speed of thirty-two mph. But there was a lot of talk in U.S. naval circles that her armour would leave her somewhat underprotected, and the wrangle led in 1937 to the introduction of yet another new battleship class, *South Dakota*, a design featuring many improvements over the *North Carolina* design, all resulting in a very considerable weight saving. *South Dakota* would prove to be a lighter, better protected solution with about the same performance as that of *North Carolina*, and many of her virtues would ultimately influence the design of *Iowa*, the final fast battleship class.

The *Iowa* class battleships were ordered by the U.S. Navy in 1939 and 1940 to escort the new fast-carrier task forces that would be operating in the Pacific Theater of the Second World War. Six of the battleships were planned and ordered; four were built, but the two others, USS *Illinois* and USS *Kentucky*, were laid down but cancelled at the end of the war. The *Iowa*s were the longest battleships ever built.

The *Iowa*s took part in four American-involved wars. Their primary roles in the Second World War were defending the U.S. aircraft carriers and shelling enemy positions. They maintained artillery support for United Nations forces during the Korean War. During the Vietnam War, the *New Jersey* shelled Viet Cong and the Viet Nam People's Army forces. In the 1980s, the *Missouri* and *Wisconsin* operated in Operation Desert Storm, firing missiles and shelling Iraqi targets.

These big warships have earned their keep in the various conflicts since the 1940s, but they have

The USS *Missouri* firing her nine main guns in salvo during the 1991 Gulf War.

been costly to operate and maintain. With the ending of the Cold War, and the subsequent defence drawdown, all four of the *Iowa* class ships were decommissioned and removed from the Naval Vessel Register. Later, however, the U.S. Congress, concerned that the existing naval gunfire support would not be sufficient for amphibious operations, insisted that the Navy resinstate two of the BBs. That led to a prolonged debate about whether battleships should continue to have a role in the modern navy. Finally, all four of the vessels were stricken from the Register and were released for donation to non-profit organizations. All are now oart of non-profit maritime museums in the United States.

The general characteristics of the *Iowa* class battleships include an overall length of 861 feet, a beam of 108 feet, a draught of thirty-six feet, a top speed of thirty-six mph, and a range of 11,700 miles at twenty-three mph. During the Korean War period, the ship's complement numbered 2,700 officers and men; in the 1980s it was reduced to 1,800 officers and men. The armament included nine sixteen-inch 50 calibre Mark 7 main guns, twenty five-inch guns, eighty 40mm Bofors guns, 49 20mm Oerlikon guns. In the Cold War years, the armament included nine sixteen-inch main guns, twelve five-inch guns, thirty-two Tomahawk missiles, sixteen Harpoon missiles, four 20mm Phalanx gun systems.

The sixteen-inch main guns, which fired either armour-piercing or high-explosive shells over a range of up to twenty miles, and at a firing rate of two rounds per minute per gun, rested within armoured turrets, three guns to a turret with only the top of the turret protruding above the main deck. Each turret extended either four or five decks down, the lower spaces containing rooms for storing and handling projectiles and powder bags to fire them. Each of the turrets was operated by a crew of 85 to 110 men and the guns could be fired independently, in any combination, or in a broadside nine-gun salvo.

The *Iowa*s also carried ten twin-mounted five-inch 38-calibre guns, a type which was added to the majority of American warships in the Second World War, as they proved extemely reliable, robust, and highly accurate. It was a dual-purpose gun able to fire at both surface and air targets with considerable success, and had roughly twice the effective range of the five-inch gun it had replaced in the anti-aircraft role. Some of these mounts were removed during the modifications of the 1980s to make room for the armoured box launchers that carried the Tomahawk missiles used in the 1991 Gulf War.

The *Iowa* class battleships were protected with heavy armour against bombs and shell fire, as well as substantial underwater protection against torpedoes. Based largely on the armour protection of the previous *South Dakota* class, the *Iowa* armour was designed to provide immunity against sixteen-inch guns at distances of between 18,000 and 30,000 yards. Protection for the magazines and engine rooms included an armour belt 12.2-inches thick, sloped to 13.5-inches. Both the *Missouri* and *Wisconsin* were fitted with 14.5-inch vertical armour on the forward armoured bulkhead, the conning tower, and the turret barbettes, for added protection from fire directly ahead, a threat considered likely due to the high speed of the *Iowa* class ships.

For torpedo defence, each side of the ship was protected by two tanks mounted below the waterline outside the armour belt and separated by a bulkhead. The outer hull was intended to detonate a torpedo, the two outer compartments absorbing the shock, with splinters and debris stopped by the armour belt and the empty compartment behind. The system, like the rest of the armour protection on the class, was less effective than intended, especially in withstanding the effects of aerial bombing during the Pacific campaign.

At the time of their commissioning, the *Iowa* battleships were each equipped with two aircraft cat-

left: The breech of a sixteen-inch main gun in the Japanese battleship *Nagato* in August 1945; below: Crewmen of the USS *Missouri* stripping paint from the main guns of their ship while returning to the Pacific coast of the United States, October 1945.

above: The *New Jersey* late in WW2; right: *Iowa* ploughing through a heavy sea in 1946; far right: American battleship sailors relaxing.

apults for the launching of floatplanes, initially the Curtiss SC Seahawk and the Vought OS2U King-fisher, used in a spotting capacity for the main gun batteries of the ship and, secondarily, on search and rescue missions. In the Korean War, the floatplanes had been replaced by helicopters.

After the 1991 Gulf War, and the dissolution of the former Soviet Union, began a programme of de-commissioning and mothballing many of the warships it had activated from its reserve fleet in the ear-lier effort to develop a 600-ship navy, which had included fifteen aircraft carriers, four battleships, more than 100 submarines, and many examples of other types. With the demise of the Soviet Union, the Navy elected to reorganize into a new 313-ship force. At that point it decided to deactivate the four recommissioned *Iowa* class battleships and return them to the reserve fleet. This was when the popular movement began for reinstating the ships to the Naval Vessel Register, and the Congress de-manded that the Navy reinstate two of the battleships to the Register and maintain them within the mothball fleet until the Navy could certify that it had sufficient gunfire support for amphibious oper-ations within the current fleet requirement, to meet or exceed that provided by the capability of the battleships. Though all four of the Iowas have now been officially struck from the Register, they will not be scrapped and have been donated for use as museum ships.

The USS *Iowa* (BB-61) was dispatched to Argentia Bay, Newfoundland, in August 1943, to deal with the German battleship *Tirpitz* in the event that warship raider should break out of her station in Nor-way and threaten the Allied Atlantic convoys. Her next assignment was to bring President Roosevelt to Cairo and Tehran for the war meetings with Prime Minister Churchill and Premier Stalin. She sailed in January 1944 to the Pacific and the Marshall Islands campaign. In late January she served by screen-ing the Task Force 58 aircraft carriers during their air strikes on Truk, Kwajalein, and Eniwetok Islands. In February, *Iowa* supported the carrier air strikes against Guam, Rota, Tinian and Saipan. In March she was assigned to bombard Mili Atoll in the Marshall Islands and while there was hit by two enemy shells which caused minor damage. In April she was working in support of American landings on Hollandia in New Guinea. By 1 May *Iowa* was bombarding Ponape Island in the Carolines. Six weeks later she was lobbing her shells onto Saipan and Tinian in the Marianas, before heading off to participate in the Battle of the Philippine Sea. Into the summer, she was a part of Task Force 38 in strikes on Iwo Jima and Chichijima, and then onto the landings at Peleliu in September.

On 10 October, *Iowa* was in support of the carrier air strikes on Formosa and the Ryuku Islands before moving on to support air strikes against Luzon ahead of the landings at Leyte Gulf on 20 Oc-tober. Following that action she returned to San Francisco for a refit, remaining there until March 1945. From mid-April she worked with the carriers in support of their strikes on Okinawa. She was covering carrier air strikes against the southern Japanese home island of Kyushu between 25 May and 13 June in preparation for the Allied invasion of Japan. With the end of the Pacific war, *Iowa* was pres-ent in Tokyo Bay for the official surrender ceremony conducted on her sister ship, the *Missouri* on 2 September.

The second battleship of the *Iowa* class, the USS *New Jersey* (BB-62) was launched a year to the day after the Japanese surprise attack on U.S. Navy ships and facilities at Pearl Harbor, Hawaii. It was not until January 1944 that she first saw action, as part of Task Group 58 when she took part in a screen-ing operation for the carriers *Bunker Hill*, *Cowpens,* and *Monterey* as they launched air strikes against

U.S. Army General Douglas MacArthur signing the Japanese surrender documents on board the *Missouri* in Tokyo Bay, 2 September 1945.

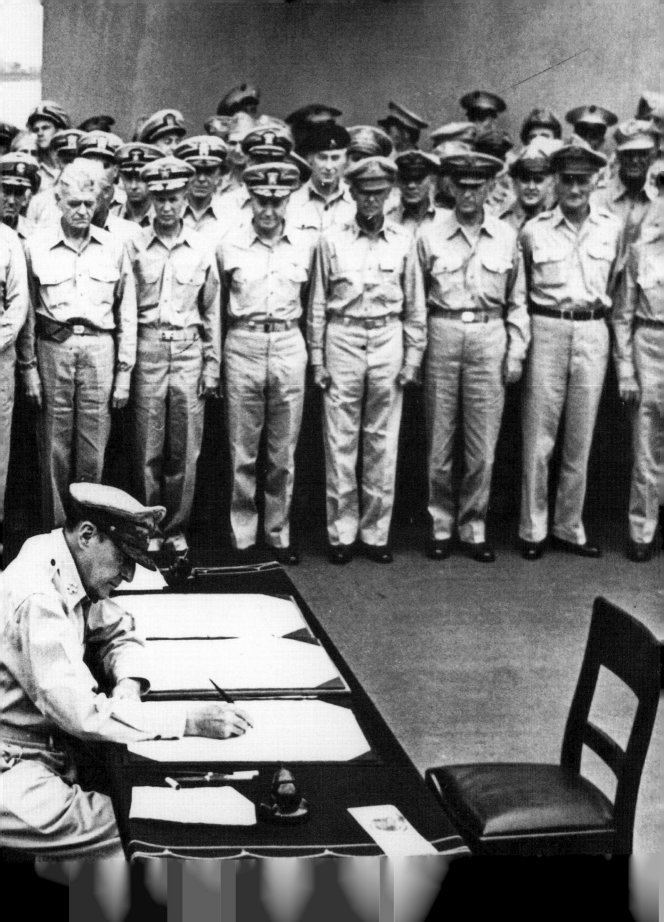

Kwajalein and Eniwetok. The first firing of her main gun battery took place on 17 February when she engaged two Japanese destroyers and two trawlers, one of which she sank. In April, the *New Jersey* was involved in the bombardment of Mili, in covering the air strikes against the Palau Islands, and the landings at Hollandia, as well as joining with six other battleships in shelling Ponape. In June she bombarded Saipan and Tinian in the Marianas chain.

Operating out of the massive U.S. fleet anchorage at Ulithi from 28 August, she covered carrier air strikes against various islands in the Philippines before the battle for Leyte in which she joined in attacks on the island of Luzon. For most of September she screened carrier air strikes against targets in Indo-China, Luzon, Formosa, and Okinawa. By May 1945, *New Jersey* was in the Puget Sound Navy Yard for a refit and in August was bombarding Wake Island while on her way back to the western Pacific to become the flagship of the U.S. 5th Fleet at Guam near the end of the war.

On 9 December 1944, the USS *Wisconsin* (BB-64) arrived at the Pacific Fleet anchorage in Ulithi. The *Wisconsin* became part of the U.S. 3rd Fleet and took part in attacks on Luzon in the Philippines in late December, before helping cover the fast carrier air strikes on Formosa and the Pescadores. She then bombarded targets near Tokyo in mid-February before sailing on to Iwo Jima to assist there in the bombardment ahead of the landings on the 19th. From Iwo she went on to attack targets on the main Japanese island of Honshu before taking part in the Okinawa campaign and then going back to Japan to bombard targets in areas near Kobe and Kure. She returned for another session bombarding Okinawa lasting into May. After a period of repairs in the Philippines, *Wisconsin* was replenished and left on her final assignment of the war, a return to Japan in support of more carrier air strikes through the end of the war in mid-August.

BB-63, the USS *Missouri*, was the last of the *Iowas* and the last of the last battleships. Carrying the flag of Vice Admiral Marc Mitscher, the *Missouri* sailed to the western Pacific Fleet Anchorage at Ulithi in the Caroline Islands, arriving on 13 January 1945. As part of Task Force 58, she participated in the fast-carrier air strikes against Tokyo and Yokohama in February, prior to supporting the American landings on Iwo Jima, followed by a strike in March on the Japanese island of Kyushu. On 24 March she joined other U.S. Navy battleships in the bombardment of Okinawa and was part of the carrier group that attacked and sank the Japanese battleship *Yamato*, the largest battleship ever built and the pride of the Imperial Japanese Navy.

On 11 April, the *Missouri* was hit by a 'Zeke' kamikaze aircraft which struck her on the starboard side below the main deck level and abreast of her number three turret. Former Seaman First Class Anthony Alessandro: "He was wave-skimming. We hit that plane with everything we had. I don't know how he got through all of that flak." Somehow the Japanese pilot drove his fighter into the side of the *Missouri*, killing himself and starting a fire that was soon contained and extinguished. None of the ship's crew were killed and the damage to the ship was minor. The next day, the ship's chaplain held a brief funeral service for the Japanese pilot, which was boycotted by some of the crew who refused to be part of a ceremony for the enemy. The *Missouri* was again subjected to attack by a kamikaze aircraft less than a week later. After being hit many times by anti-aircraft gunfire from the battleship, the plane missed most of the big warship before managing to clip some machinery on the fantail before plummeting into her wake. When the aircraft disintegrated on impact, some metal bits flew up and injured two sailors.

By the end of April, the battleship was again screening carrier air strikes against Okinawa and then against the Japanese home island of Kyushu, a practice she was involved with until the end of the war in August.

The *Missouri* was chosen to be the site of the official surrender signing ceremony to be held on the morning of 2 September. The ship lay in Tokyo Bay as the American General Douglas MacArthur addressed the crew and the dignitaries: "We are gathered here, representatives of the major warring powers, to conclude a solemn agreement whereby peace may be restored. The issues involving divergent ideas and ideologies, have been determined on the battlefields and hence are not for our discussiuon or our debate. It is my earnest hope and indeed the hope of all mankind that from this solemn occasion a better world shall emerge out of the blood and carnage of the past. Let us pray that peace be now restored to the world and that God will preserve it always. These proceedings are closed."

Soviet Fleet Admiral Sergei Gorshkov, on seeing the USS *Iowa* during a NATO exercise in 1985: "You Americans do not realize what formidable warships you have in these four battleships. We have concluded after careful analysis that these magnificent vessels are in fact the most to be feared in your entire naval arsenal. When engaged in combat we could throw everything we have at those ships and all our firepower would just bounce off or be of little effect. Then we are exhausted, we will detect you coming over the horizon and then you will sink us."

The USS *Missouri*

The Japanese naval air attack on U.S. battleships in Pearl Harbor, Hawaii, on 7 December 1941 brought the United States into the Second World War the next day.